★ World War I ★

Primary Sources

Edited by James D. Torr

Lucent Books,   Diego, CA 92127

Titles in the American War Library series include:

World War II
Hitler and the Nazis
Kamikazes
Leaders and Generals
Life as a POW
Life of an American Soldier in
  Europe
Strategic Battles in Europe
Strategic Battles in the Pacific
The War at Home
Weapons of War

The Civil War
Leaders of the North and South
Life Among the Soldiers and
  Cavalry
Lincoln and the Abolition of
  Slavery
Strategic Battles
Weapons of War

Library of Congress Cataloging-in-Publication Data

Torr, James D., 1974–
  American war library, World War I: primary sources /
by James D. Torr.
      p. cm. — (American war library. World War I)
Includes bibliographical references and index.
Summary: Presents the original documents used for the American
War Library, World War I series.
  ISBN 1-59018-008-9 (alk. paper)
  1. World War, 1914–1918—Juvenile literature. 2. World War,
1914–1918—Sources. [1. World War, 1914–1918—Sources.]
I. Title. II. Series.
  D522.7 .T67 2002
  940.3—dc21

2001005790

✯ **Contents** ✯

A Nation Forged by War

The United States, like many nations, was forged and defined by war. Despite Benjamin Franklin's opinion that "There never was a good war or a bad peace," the United States owes its very existence to the War of Independence, one to which Franklin wholeheartedly subscribed. The country forged by war in 1776 was tempered and made stronger by the Civil War in the 1860s.

The Texas Revolution, the Mexican-American War, and the Spanish-American War expanded the country's borders and gave it overseas possessions. These wars made the United States a world power, but this status came with a price, as the nation became a key but reluctant player in both World War I and World War II.

Each successive war further defined the country's role on the world stage. Following World War II, U.S. foreign policy redefined itself to focus on the role of defender, not only of the freedom of its own citizens, but also of the freedom of people everywhere. During the cold war that followed World War II until the collapse of the Soviet Union, defending the world meant fighting communism. This goal, manifested in the Korean and Vietnam conflicts, proved elusive, and soured the American public on its achievability. As the United States emerged as the world's sole superpower, American foreign policy has been guided less by national interest and more on protecting international human rights. But as involvement in Somalia and Kosovo prove, this goal has been equally elusive.

As a result, the country's view of itself changed. Bolstered by victories in World Wars I and II, Americans first relished the role of protector. But, as war followed war in a seemingly endless procession, Americans began to doubt their leaders, their motives, and themselves. The Vietnam War especially caused people to question the validity of sending its young people to die in places where they were not particularly wanted and for people who did not seem especially grateful.

While the most obvious changes brought about by America's wars have been geopolitical in nature, many other aspects of society have been touched. War often does not bring about change directly, but acts instead like the catalyst in a chemical reaction, accelerating changes already in progress.

Some of these changes have been societal. The role of women in the United States had been slowly changing, but World War II put thousands into the workforce and into uniform. They might have gone back to being housewives after the war, but equality, once experienced, would not be forgotten.

Likewise, wars have accelerated technological change. The necessity for faster airplanes and a more destructive bomb led to the development of jet planes and nuclear energy. Artificial fibers developed for parachutes in the 1940s were used in the clothing of the 1950s.

Lucent Books' American War Library covers key wars in the development of the nation. Each war is covered in several volumes, to allow for more detail, context, and to provide volumes on often neglected subjects, such as the kamikazes of World War II, or weapons used in the Civil War. As with all Lucent Books, notes, annotated bibliographies, and appendixes such as glossaries give students a launching point for further research. In addition, sidebars and archival photographs enhance the text. Together, each volume in The American War Library will aid students in understanding how America's wars have shaped and changed its politics, economics, and society.

Chapter 1

The Road to War

In August 1914, when fighting broke out in Europe following the assassination of Archduke Franz Ferdinand, the idea that the United States would send soldiers across the Atlantic Ocean to fight in a European war was unthinkable to most Americans. President Woodrow Wilson proclaimed the United States' neutrality in the war, and many Americans opposed U.S. involvement.

The spark that ignited World War I was the June 28, 1914, assassination of Archduke Franz Ferdinand, heir to the throne of Austria-Hungary, by a Serbian terrorist. One reason that this single incident embroiled all the great powers of Europe in war was the system of alliances that existed in Europe at the time. In what was known as the Dual Alliance, Austria-Hungary and Germany had committed to fighting together if either nation were attacked by Russia. Russia, meanwhile, was allied with France, and also viewed itself as a protector of Serbia. Great Britain, although not for-

The assassination of Austrian archduke Franz Ferdinand, the event that brought on World War I.

mally bound by treaty, was diplomatically and strategically aligned with Russia and France. Therefore, as Austria-Hungary confronted Serbia about the assassination, the

Central Powers (Austria-Hungary and Germany) lined up against the Allied Powers (Great Britain, France, and Russia).

The United States was not officially tied to these European alliances. However, the United States did have a strong economic interest in Europe. At the start of the war American industries were shipping millions of dollars in exports to both the Allied and Central Powers. But by 1916 Great Britain's naval blockade of the Central Powers had effectively ended U.S. trade with Germany.

Despite Americans' desire to remain neutral and avoid involvement in a foreign war, U.S. economic prosperity had become heavily dependent on trade with the Allies. And Germany objected to the American shipments of arms and other supplies to Great Britain, saying they contradicted American neutrality. Ultimately, Germany's attempts to stop these shipments would only worsen U.S.-German relations.

Great Britain's naval superiority meant that Germany had to rely on surprise submarine attacks. In 1915, Germany declared a war zone around the British Isles and began sinking passenger and merchant ships in the area, some of which had Americans on board. Germany temporarily halted these attacks in response to American protests, but its resumption of submarine warfare in January 1917 was a major reason the United States entered the war.

The final, decisive factor was the March 1917 release of the Zimmerman telegram, a message intercepted by British agents in which Germany proposed a Ger-

A British merchant ship struggles to stay afloat after being hit by a German torpedo.

man-Mexican military alliance against the United States. The threat of bringing hostilities to American soil outraged the nation, and on April 2, 1917, Wilson asked Congress for a declaration of war against Germany. Four days later, America entered World War I.

The Dual Alliance

In 1879, Germany and Austria-Hungary pledged to defend each other should either of the two nations be attacked by their common enemy, Russia. Under Article 2 of the treaty, each nation may remain neutral if its ally engages in a war with a country other than Russia but is bound to defend its ally if Russia enters the conflict in any way. Although the treaty they signed was secret, the rest of Europe was aware of the general terms of the agreement, and it became known as the Dual Alliance.

ARTICLE 1. Should, contrary to their hope, and against the loyal desire of the two High Contracting Parties [Germany and Austria-Hungary], one of the two Empires be attacked by Russia the High Contracting Parties are bound to come to the assistance of the other with the whole war strength of their Empires, and accordingly only to conclude peace together and upon mutual agreement.

ARTICLE 2. Should one of the High Contracting Parties be attacked by another Power, the other High Contracting Party binds itself hereby, not only not to support

the aggressor against its high Ally, but to observe at least a benevolent neutral attitude towards its fellow Contracting Party.

Should, however, the attacking party in such a case be supported by Russia, either by an active cooperation or by military measures which constitute a menace to the Party attacked, then the obligation stipulated in Article 1 of this Treaty, for reciprocal assistance with the whole fighting force, becomes equally operative, and the conduct of the war by the two High Contracting Parties shall in this case also be in common until the conclusion of a common peace.

ARTICLE 3. The duration of this Treaty shall be provisionally fixed at five years from the day of ratification. One year before the expiration of this period the two High Contracting Parties shall consult together concerning the question whether the conditions serving as the basis of the Treaty still prevail, and reach an agreement in regard to the further continuance or possible modification of certain details. If in the course of the first month of the last year of the Treaty no invitation has been received from either side to open these negotiations, the Treaty shall be considered as renewed for a further period of three years.

ARTICLE 4. This Treaty shall, in conformity with its peaceful character, and to avoid any misinterpretation, be kept secret by the two High Contracting Parties, and only communicated to a third Power upon a joint understanding between the two Parties, and according to the terms of a special Agreement.

The two High Contracting Parties venture to hope, after the sentiments expressed by the [Russian] Emperor Alexander [who declared that Russia did not intend any attacks on Germany or Austria-Hungary] at the meeting at Alexandrovo, that the armaments [armies] of Russia will not in reality prove to be menacing to them, and have on that account no reason for making a communication at present; should, however, this hope, contrary to their expectations, prove to be erroneous [false], the two High Contracting Parties would consider it their loyal obligation to let the Emperor Alexander know, at least confidentially, that they must consider an attack on either of them as directed against both.

ARTICLE 5. This Treaty shall derive its validity from the approbation [approval] of the two Exalted Sovereigns [Kaiser Wilhelm of Germany and Emperor Franz Josef of Austria-Hungary] and shall be ratified within fourteen days after this approbation has been granted by Their Most Exalted Majesties. In witness whereof the Plenipotentiaries [diplomatic representatives] have signed this Treaty with their own hands and affixed their arms.

Done at Vienna, October 7, 1879

The Dual Alliance, secret treaty between the German Empire and the Austro-Hungarian Empire, signed October 7, 1879.

Austria's emperor Franz Josef I (left) and King Wilhelm I of Prussia signed a secret treaty guaranteeing mutual aid in case of attack by Russia.

The Franco-Russian Alliance Military Convention

France and Germany share a border, and control of border provinces has historically been a cause for war between the two nations. After Germany allied itself with Austria-Hungary, France sought to balance the power of the Dual Alliance with an alliance of its own. France found Russia, which feared that the Dual Alliance might try to expand to the east. In 1894 France and Russia formalized their alliance in the document reprinted below.

France and Russia, being animated [motivated] by a common desire to preserve peace, and having no other object than to meet the necessities of a defensive war, provoked by an attack of the forces of the Triple Alliance [a revised version of the Dual Alliance that included Italy] against either of them, have agreed upon the following provisions:

1. If France is attacked by Germany, or by Italy supported by Germany, Russia shall employ all her available forces to attack Germany.

If Russia is attacked by Germany, or by Austria supported by Germany, France shall employ all her available forces to attack Germany.

2. In case the forces of the Triple Alliance, or of any one of the Powers belonging to it, should be mobilized [brought into readiness for war], France and Russia, at the first news of this event and without previous agreement being necessary, shall mobilize immediately and simultaneously the whole of their forces, and shall transport them as far as possible to their frontiers [borders with their enemy].

3. The available forces to be employed against Germany shall be, on the part of France, 1,300,000 men, on the part of Russia, 700,000 or 800,000 men.

These forces shall engage to the full [go to war] with such speed that Germany will have to fight simultaneously on the East and on the West.

4. The General Staffs [leaders] of the Armies of the two countries shall cooperate with each other at all times in the preparation and facilitation of the execution of the measures mentioned above.

They shall communicate with each other, while there is still peace, all information relative to the armies of the Triple Alliance which is already in their possession or shall come into their possession.

Ways and means of corresponding in time of war shall be studied and worked out in advance.

5. France and Russia shall not conclude [negotiate] peace separately.

6. The present Convention shall have the same duration as the Triple Alliance.

7. All the clauses enumerated above shall be kept absolutely secret.

Franco-Russian Alliance Military Convention, secret treaty between France and Russia, signed August 18, 1892.

The German Request for Free Passage Through Belgium

As soon as Germany decided to go to war against Russia and France, the country set into motion the war plan it had prepared well in advance—the Schlieffen Plan. The Schlieffen Plan called for Germany to draw French forces forward in the Alsace-Lorraine region of Germany, along the French border. As French forces committed themselves to battle in this region, the main German force would cross the countries of Luxembourg and Belgium and begin entering France all along its northeastern border. However, Germany could not simply invade and conquer Belgium without angering public opinion in foreign countries. More importantly, Germany did not want England to become involved in the war, yet they knew that England would not stand by as Germany invaded Belgium. In order to create the appearance that they were behaving according to international law that required combatants to respect the rights of neutral countries, German diplomats made a formal request to enter Belgium. That request, reprinted below, was made by the German ambassador at Brussels, Herr von Below Saleske, on August 2, 1914.

Reliable information has been received by the German Government to the effect that French forces intend to march on the line

German troops wait at a staging area on the Belgian border.

of the Meuse [River] by Givet and Namur. This information leaves no doubt as to the intention of France to march through Belgian territory against Germany.

The German Government cannot but fear that Belgium, in spite of the utmost goodwill, will be unable, without assistance, to repel so considerable a French invasion with sufficient prospect of success to afford an adequate guarantee against danger to Germany. It is essential for the self-defence of Germany that she should anticipate any such hostile attack. The German Government would, however, feel the deepest regret if Belgium regarded as an act of hostility against herself the fact that the measures of Germany's opponents force Germany, for her own protection, to enter Belgian territory.

In order to exclude any possibility of misunderstanding, the German Government make the following declaration: —

1. Germany has in view no act of hostility against Belgium. In the event of Belgium being prepared in the coming war to maintain an attitude of friendly neutrality towards Germany, the German Government bind them selves, at the conclusion of peace, to guarantee the possessions and independence of the Belgian Kingdom in full.

2. Germany undertakes, under the above-mentioned condition, to evacuate Belgian territory on the conclusion of peace.

3. If Belgium adopts a friendly attitude, Germany is prepared, in cooperation with the Belgian authorities, to purchase all necessaries for her troops against a cash payment, and to pay an indemnity [cash] for any damage that may have been caused by German troops.

4. Should Belgium oppose the German troops, and in particular should she throw difficulties in the way of their march by a resistance of the fortresses on the Meuse [River], or by destroying railways, roads, tunnels, or other similar works, Germany will, to her regret, be compelled to consider Belgium as an enemy.

In this event, Germany can undertake no obligations towards Belgium, but the eventual adjustment of the relations between the two States must be left to the decision of arms [winner of the war].

The German Government, however, entertain the distinct hope that this eventuality will not occur, and that the Belgian Government will know how to take the necessary measures to prevent the occurrence of incidents such as those mentioned. In this case the friendly ties which bind the two neighbouring States will grow stronger and more enduring.

The German Request for Free Passage Through Belgium, delivered August 2, 1914.

Belgium's Reply to Germany

Belgium vehemently refused Germany's request to pass through the country in order to invade France. Belgian minister of foreign affairs M. Davignon delivered Belgium's reply, reprinted below, on August 3, 1914. Belgian troops resisted when Germany crossed its borders the following day, but by August 20, the German army had occupied the Belgian city of Brussels.

This note [asking free passage] has made a deep and painful impression upon the Belgian Government. The intentions attributed to France by Germany are in contradiction to the formal declarations made to us on August 1, in the name of the French Government. Moreover, if, contrary to our expectation, Belgian neutrality should be violated by France, Belgium intends to fulfil her international obligations and the Belgian army would offer the most vigorous resistance to the invader. The treaties of 1839, confirmed by the treaties of 1870 [which guaranteed the independence of Belgium],

vouch for the independence and neutrality of Belgium under the guarantee of the Powers [France, Germany, England, and Austria-Hungary], and notably of the Government of His Majesty the King of Prussia [the formal title of Germany's Kaiser Wilhelm II].

Belgium has always been faithful to her international obligations, she has carried out her duties in a spirit of loyal impartiality, and she has left nothing undone to maintain and enforce respect for her neutrality.

The attack upon her independence with which the German Government threaten her constitutes a flagrant violation of international law. No strategic interest justifies such a violation of law.

German troops march into Belgium's capital of Brussels in 1914.

The Belgian Government, if they were to accept the proposals submitted to them, would sacrifice the honour of the nation and betray their duty towards Europe.

Conscious of the part which Belgium has played for more than eighty years in the civilisation of the world, they refuse to believe that the independence of Belgium can only be preserved at the price of the violation of her neutrality.

If this hope is disappointed the Belgian Government are firmly resolved to repel, by all the means in their power, every attack upon their rights.

Belgium's Response to the Request for Passage, August 3, 1914.

Former U.S. president William Howard Taft advocated American neutrality in World War I.

Initial American Reaction to the Outbreak of War in Europe

When World War I began in Europe in August 1914, most Americans were shocked but also relieved that the war was thousands of miles away from them. In an article for Independent *magazine, former president William Howard Taft (who left office in 1913) expressed the popular view that the outbreak of war was tragic and the hope that the United States could stay out of the conflict.*

As I write, Germany is reported to have declared war against Russia and France, and the participation of England on the one side and of Italy on the other seems imminent. Nothing like it has occurred since the great Napoleonic wars, and with modern armaments and larger populations nothing has occurred like it since the world began.

It is a cataclysm. It is a retrograde step in Christian civilization. It will be difficult to keep the various countries of the Balkans out of the war, and Greece and Turkey may take part in it. All Europe is to be a battleground. It is reported that the neutrality of Holland has already been ignored and Belgium offers such opportunities in the campaigns certain to follow that her territory, too, will be the scene of struggle.

War and Commerce

Private property and commercial shipping under an enemy's flag are subject to capture and appropriation by prize proceedings and with the formidable navies of England, France, Germany, Russia and Italy active[,] the great carrying trade of the world will be in large part suspended or destroyed or will be burdened with such heavy insurance as greatly to curtail it.

The commerce of the world makes much for the prosperity of the countries with whom it is conducted and its interruption means great inconvenience and economic suffering among all people, whether at peace or war. The capital which the European people have invested by the billions in the United States, Canada, Australia, South Africa and in the Orient must perforce be withdrawn to fill the war chests of the nations engaged in a death grapple, and the enterprises which that capital made possible are likely to be greatly crippled while the hope of any further expansion must be definitely given up.

This general European war will give a feverish activity in a number of branches of our industry, but on the whole we shall suffer with the rest of the world, except that we shall not be destroying or blowing up our existing wealth or sacrificing the lives of our best young men and youth.

It is hard to prophesy the scope of a war like this because history offers no precedent. It is impossible to foresee the limits of a war of any proportions when confined only to two countries. In our own small Spanish war we began it to free Cuba and when the war closed we found ourselves ten thousand miles away with the Philippines on our hands.

The immense waste of life and treasure in a modern war makes the loss to the conqueror only less, if indeed it be less, than the loss to the conquered.

With a high patriotic spirit, people enter upon war with confidence and with the thought of martial glory and success. The sacrifices they have to make, the suffering they have to undergo are generally such that if victory does not rest upon their banners[,] they seek a scapegoat for that which they themselves have brought on in the head of the state, and the king or emperor who begins a war or allows one to begin puts at stake not only the prestige of his nation but also the stability and integrity of his dynasty.

In such a war as this, therefore, with the universal tendency to popular control in every country, the strain and defeat in war may lead to a state of political flux in those countries which shall suffer defeat, with all the attendant difficulties and disorder that a change of government involves.

While we can be sure that such a war as this, taking it by and large, will be a burden upon the United States and is a great misfortune, looked at solely from the standpoint of the United States, we have every reason to be happy that we are able to preserve strict neutrality in respect to it. Within our hospitable boundaries we have living prosperous and contented emigrants in large numbers from all the countries who are to take part in the war and the sympathies of these people will of course be with their respective native lands. Were there no other reason this circumstance would tend to keep us free from an entanglement.

We may sincerely hope that Japan will not be involved. She will not be unless the war is carried on to the far Orient, to India or to China. Germany has but a small settlement in the Orient, while France and Russia and England would be allies in this war and it would seem quite unlikely that there would arise any obligation under the English-Japanese alliance for Japan to assist England.

Of the great powers of the world, therefore, the only ones left out are likely to be the United States and Japan, and perhaps only the United States, by reason of the alliance between Japan and England. Japan, if she keeps out of the war, will occupy the same advantageous position, which will be ours, of complete neutrality, of an actually judicial attitude, and therefore, of having an opportunity at some time, we may hope, to mediate between the powers and to help to mitigate this disaster to mankind.

The Future of War

At the time when so many friends of peace have thought that we were making real progress toward the abolition of war this sudden outbreak of the greatest war in history is most discouraging. The future looks dark indeed, but we should not despair.

"God moves in a mysterious way His wonders to perform." Now that the war is a settled fact, we must hope that some good may come from this dreadful scourge. The armaments of Europe had been growing heavier and heavier, bankruptcy has stared many of the nations in the face, conflict between races had begun to develop.

War seemed likely at some stage and the question which each country had to answer for itself was at what time the situation would be most favorable for its success. The immediate participants have decided that the time has come and through their international alliance all Europe is involved.

There has been no real test of the heavy armament on land or water as developed by modern invention and this contest is to show what has been well spent for war purposes and what has been wasted. It is by no means certain that waste will not exceed in cost that which was spent to effective purpose.

One thing I think we can reasonably count on is that with the prostration of industry, with the blows of prosperity, with the state of flux that is likely to follow this titanic struggle, there will be every opportunity for common sense to resume its sway; and after the horrible expenditure of the blood of the best and the savings of the rich and the poor, the opportunity and the motive for a reduction of armament and the taking away of a temptation to further war will be greatly enhanced.

It is an awful remedy, but in the end it may be worth what it costs, if it makes this the last great war. The influence of America can be thrown most effectively for peace when peace is possible and for minimum armaments when disaster and exhaustion shall make the contending peoples and their rulers see things as they are.

William Howard Taft, "A Message to the People of the United States," *Independent*, vol. 79 (1914), pp. 198–99.

Wilson's Appeal for Neutrality

Shortly after World War I began in Europe, President Woodrow Wilson issued this call to the American people to remain neutral in thought and action.

My fellow countrymen: I suppose that every thoughtful man in America has asked himself, during these last troubled weeks, what influence the European war may exert upon the United States, and I take the liberty of addressing a few words to you in order to point out that it is entirely within our own choice what its effects upon us will be and to urge very earnestly upon you the sort of speech and conduct which will best safeguard the Nation against distress and disaster.

The effect of the war upon the United States will depend upon what American citizens say and do. Every man who really loves America will act and speak in the true spirit of neutrality, which is the spirit of impartiality and fairness and friendliness to all concerned. The spirit of the Nation in this critical matter will be determined largely by what individuals and society and those gathered in public meetings do and say, upon what newspapers and magazines contain, upon what ministers utter in their pulpits, and men proclaim as their opinions on the street.

The people of the United States are drawn from many nations, and chiefly from the nations now at war. It is natural and inevitable that there should be the

President Woodrow Wilson urged Americans to remain calm and impartial.

utmost variety of sympathy and desire among them with regard to the issues and circumstances of the conflict. Some will wish one nation, others another, to succeed in the momentous struggle. It will be easy to excite passion and difficult to allay [alleviate] it. Those responsible for exciting it will assume a heavy responsibility, responsibility for no less a thing than that the people of the United States, whose love of their country and whose loyalty to its Government should unite them as Americans all, bound in honor and affection to think first of her and her interests, may be divided in camps of hostile opinion, hot against each other, involved in the war itself in impulse and opinion if not in action.

Such divisions amongst us would be fatal to our peace of mind and might seriously stand in the way of the proper performance of our duty as the one great nation at peace, the one people holding itself ready to play a part of impartial mediation and speak the counsels of peace and accommodation, not as a partisan, but as a friend.

I venture, therefore, my fellow countrymen, to speak a solemn word of warning to you against that deepest, most subtle, most essential breach of neutrality which may spring out of partisanship, out of passionately taking sides. The United States must be neutral in fact as well as in name during these days that are to try men's souls. We must be impartial in thought as well as in action, must put a curb upon our sentiments as well as upon every transaction that might be construed as a preference of one party to the struggle before another.

My thought is of America. I am speaking, I feel sure, the earnest wish and purpose of every thoughtful American that this great country of ours, which is, of course, the first in our thoughts and in our hearts, should show herself in this time of peculiar trial a Nation fit beyond others to exhibit the fine poise of undisturbed judgment, the dignity of self-control, the efficiency of dispassionate action; a Nation that neither sits in judgment upon others nor is disturbed in her own counsels and which keeps herself fit and free to do what is honest and disinterested and truly serviceable for the peace of the world.

Shall we not resolve to put upon ourselves the restraints which will bring to our people the happiness and the great and lasting influence for peace we covet for them?

U.S. Senate. President Woodrow Wilson speaking to the Senate, Senate Doc. 566, 63rd Cong., 2nd sess., August 19, 1914.

The Status of Armed Merchant Vessels

During the first years of the war, a key point of contention between the United States and Germany was whether merchant vessels bound for Great Britain or other Allied Powers would be fired upon by German submarines. U.S. leaders argued that merchant vessels should not be

subject to attack, even though some merchant vessels were armed to protect against pirates and other criminals. To clarify the difference between military ships and armed merchant vessels, the U.S. Department of State issued this memorandum in September 1914.

A gun is mounted on an American merchant vessel so that it can defend itself from German warships and submarines.

A. A merchant vessel of belligerent nationality may carry an armament and ammunition for the sole purpose of defense without acquiring the character of a ship of war.

B. The presence of an armament and ammunition on board a merchant vessel creates a presumption that the armament is for offensive purposes, but the owners or agents may overcome this presumption by evidence showing that the vessel carries armament solely for defense.

C. Evidence necessary to establish the fact that the armament is solely for defense and will not be used offensively, whether the armament be mounted or stowed below, must be presented in each case independently at an official investigation. The result of the investigation must show conclusively that the armament is not intended for, and will not be used in, offensive operations. Indications that the armament will not be used offensively are:

1. That the caliber of the guns carried does not exceed six inches.
2. That the guns and small arms carried are few in number.
3. That no guns are mounted on the forward part of the vessel.
4. That the quantity of ammunition carried is small.
5. That the vessel is manned by its usual crew, and the officers are the same as those on board before war was declared.
6. That the vessel intends to and actually does clear for a port lying in its usual trade route, or a port indicating its purpose to continue in the same trade in which it was engaged before war was declared.
7. That the vessel takes on board fuel and supplies sufficient only to carry it to its port of destination, or the same quantity substantially which it has been accustomed to take for a voyage before war was declared.
8. That the cargo of the vessel consists of articles of commerce unsuited for the use of a ship of war in operations against an enemy.
9. That the vessel carries passengers who are as a whole unfitted to enter the military or naval service of the belligerent whose flag the vessel flies, or of any of its allies, and particularly if the passenger list includes women and children.
10. That the speed of the ship is slow.

D. Port authorities, on the arrival in a port of the United States of an armed vessel of belligerent nationality, claiming to be a merchant vessel, should immediately investigate and report to Washington on the foregoing indications as to the intended use of the armament, in order that it may be determined whether the evidence is sufficient to remove the presumption that the vessel is, and should be treated as, a ship of war. Clearance will not be granted until authorized from Washington, and the master will be so informed upon arrival.

E. The conversion of a merchant vessel into a ship of war is a question of fact which is to be established by direct or circumstantial evidence of intention to use the vessel as a ship of war.

Department of State, "The Status of Armed Merchant Vessels," September 19, 1914.

Outrage at the Sinking of the *Lusitania*

On May 7, 1915, a torpedo fired by a German submarine sank the Lusitania, *a British passenger liner, off the coast of Ireland. The attack killed 1,198 people, including 128 Americans.*

The sinking of the Lusitania *created much anti-German sentiment in the United States, since many Americans felt that the sinking of civilian ships constituted a war crime. Henry Watterson, a former congressman and editor of the Louisville, Kentucky,* Courier-Journal, *expressed his outrage in a May 1915 editorial.*

That which the *Courier-Journal* has feared—which it has been for weeks forecasting as likely to happen—has come to pass. A great ocean liner, passing peacefully to and from an American port, carrying a harmless ship's company of non-combatants, men, women and children, many of them American citizens, has, without chance of escape or time for prayer, been ruthlessly sent to the bottom of the deep and some thousand or more gone to the death, drowning and mangled by the murderous onset of a German submarine.

Truly, the nation of the Blackhand and the bloody heart [Serbia] has got in its work. It has got in its work, not upon armed antagonists in fair fight on battle front, but upon the unoffending and the helpless, sailing what has always been and should ever remain, to the peaceful and peace-loving, God's free and open sea.

Nothing in the annals of piracy can, in wanton and cruel ferocity, equal the destruction of the *Lusitania.*

But comes the query: What are we going to do about it? Are we at the mercy of the insane Hohenzollern [Wilhelm II of Germany], not only through his emissaries sending his odious system of government and debasing theories of casteism affecting superiority to our doors and proclaiming them, but bringing his war of conquest and murder across the line of our transit and travel over the high seas, which are ours to sail as we list, without let or hindrance from

Smoke billows as the Lusitania *sinks, the victim of a German submarine attack.*

man or monarch, from him or from any one on land or water?

Sovereign or Vassal?

Must we, as a people, sit down like dogs and see our laws defied, our flag flouted and our protests whistled down the wind of this lordling's majestic disdain?

Must we, as a nation, emulate at once the impotence [powerlessness] and the docility [meekness] of China, and before such proof of the contempt in which we are held by him and his, throw up our hands in entreaty and despair, saying to the insistence of autocracy, to the insolence of vanity, "Thy will is law"?

What could the President have meant when he declared that the government of the United States would hold the government of Germany to strict accountability in the event that its war zone pronunciamento [announcement] resulted in the loss of the life of a single American? How did he intend that his countrymen should understand him when he put forth his supplementary protests? Are we a sovereign [independent nation] or are we a vassal?

Please God, as all men on earth shall behold, we are a nation. Please God, as Europe and all the world shall know, we are Americans.

Too long already have we submitted to the free hand of the foreigner at home and abroad. Months ago should the Pan-German [German and Austro-Hungarian] propaganda, issuing from the German Embassy, led by the German Ambassador, erecting in the heart of our country a treasonable organization to support the German foray upon Belgium and France and to control our own domestic politics, have been ended.

[German ambassador Johann von] Bernstorff should have been severely rebuked and warned to proceed at his peril. For less [Edmond] Genet, the Frenchman, and Crampton, the Englishman, had been ordered away....

Some Good Americans

The poor and honest Germans of the United States—those who came here to better their fortunes and escape despotism [tyranny] and casteism; those who when they took out their naturalization papers, confessing republicanism and democracy, meant it; those who have no interest, part or lot, with Kaiserism, who ceased to be Germans and became Americans should be rescued alike from the teaching and contamination of the newly rich of Germans, whose dearest hope is to go home and build castles on the Rhine, and from the highbrow writers and herr doctors who worship at the shrine of the Hohenzollern, having learned their lesson from the highbrows of Heidelberg, Gottingen and Bonn.

The *Courier-Journal* will not go the length of saying that the President should convene Congress and advise it to declare against these barbarians a state of war. This may yet become necessary. Whilst actual war is not possible—Germany having no fleet we can wipe off the briny deep, nor army near enough to be met face to face and exterminated—yet we are not wholly without reprisal for the murder of our citizens and the destruction of their property. There are many German ships—at least two German men-of-war in the aggregate worth many millions of dollars—within our reach to make our losses, repudiated by Germany, whole again.

We must not act either in haste or passion. This catastrophe is too real, the flashlight it throws upon the methods and purposes of Germany is too appalling, to leave us in any doubt what awaits us as the bloody and brutal work goes on. Civilization should abjure [renounce] its neutrality. It should rise as one mighty, godlike force, and as far as its moral influence and physical appliance can be made to prevail, forbid the riot of hate and debauch [corruption] of blood that, like a madman, is running amuck among the innocent and unprotected.

Henry Watterson, "The Heart of Christ—the Sword of the Lord and Gideon," Louisville (Ky.) *Courier-Journal*, May 11, 1915, in *The Lusitania Case*. Comp. V. I. Droste. Ed. W. H. Tantum, Richmond, VA: Dietz, 1916.

The Zimmermann Telegram

In January 1917, British cryptographers, people who create and decipher secret codes, intercepted a telegram, reprinted below, from German foreign minister Arthur Zimmermann to the German am- *bassador in Mexico. The telegram outlined a plan to offer U.S. territory to Mexico in return for the Mexicans joining the German cause. The British presented the telegram to President Woodrow Wilson on February 24, and the American press published news of the telegram on March 1, 1917, causing anti-German sentiment in the United States to skyrocket.*

We [Germany] intend to begin on the first of February unrestricted submarine warfare [against all ships entering the war zone around the British Isles]. We shall endeavor in spite of this to keep the United States of America neutral. In the event of this not succeeding, we make Mexico a proposal or alliance on the following basis: make war together, make peace together, generous financial support and an understanding on our part that Mexico is to reconquer the lost territory in Texas, New Mexico, and Arizona. The settlement in detail is left to you [the German ambassador to Mexico]. You will inform the President [of Mexico] of the above most secretly as soon as the outbreak of war with the United States of America is certain and add the suggestion that he should, on his own initiative, invite Japan to immediate adherence and at the same time mediate between Japan and ourselves. Please call the President's attention to the fact that the ruthless employment of our submarines now offers the prospect of compelling England in a few months to make peace.

The Zimmermann Telegram, January 19, 1917. Decimal File, 862.20212/69 (1910–1929), General Records of the Department of State, Record Group 59.

Woodrow Wilson's Call for a Declaration of War

On January 31, 1917, Germany announced that it would resume unrestricted submarine warfare against all vessels bound for Great Britain. On the evening of April 2, 1917, President Woodrow Wilson delivered a speech, excerpted below, to a joint session of Congress asking for a declaration of war.

On the third of February last I officially laid before you [Congress] the extraordinary announcement of the Imperial German Government that on and after the first day of February it was its purpose to put aside all restraints of law or of humanity and use its submarines to sink every vessel that sought to approach either the ports of

President Woodrow Wilson asks Congress for a declaration of war against Germany on April 2, 1917.

Great Britain and Ireland or the western coasts of Europe or any of the ports controlled by the enemies of Germany within the Mediterranean. That had seemed to be the object of the German submarine warfare earlier in the war, but since April of last year the Imperial Government had somewhat restrained the commanders of its undersea craft in conformity with its promise then given to us that passenger boats should not be sunk and that due warning would be given to all other vessels which its submarines might seek to destroy, when no resistance was offered or escape attempted, and care taken that their crews were given at least a fair chance to save their lives in their open boats. The precautions taken were meager and haphazard enough, as was proved in distressing instance after instance in the progress of the cruel and unmanly business, but a certain degree of restraint was observed. The new policy has swept every restriction aside. Vessels of every kind, whatever their flag, their character, their cargo, their destination, their errand, have been ruthlessly sent to the bottom without warning and without thought of help or mercy for those on board, the vessels of friendly neutrals along with those of belligerents. Even hospital ships and ships carrying relief to the sorely bereaved and stricken people of Belgium, though the latter were provided with safe conduct through the prescribed areas by the German Government itself and were distinguished by unmistakable marks of identity, have been sunk with the same reckless lack of compassion or of principle.

I was for a little while unable to believe that such things would in fact be done by any government that had hitherto subscribed to the humane practices of civilized nations. International law had its origin in the attempt to set up some law which would be respected and observed upon the seas, where no nation had right of dominion and where lay the free highways of the world. By painful stage after stage has that law been built up, with meager enough results, indeed, after all was accomplished that could be accomplished, but always with a clear view, at least, of what the heart and conscience of mankind demanded. This minimum of right the German Government has swept aside under the plea of retaliation and necessity and because it had no weapons which it could use at sea except these which it is impossible to employ as it is employing them without throwing to the winds all scruples of humanity or of respect for the understandings that were supposed to underlie the intercourse of the world. I am not now thinking of the loss of property involved, immense and serious as that is, but only of the wanton and wholesale destruction of the lives of noncombatants, men, women, and children, engaged in pursuits which have always, even in the darkest periods of modern history, been deemed innocent and legitimate. Property can be paid for; the lives of peaceful and innocent people cannot be. The present German submarine warfare against commerce is a warfare against mankind.

It is a war against all nations. American ships have been sunk, American lives taken, in ways which it has stirred us very deeply to learn of, but the ships and people of other neutral and friendly nations have been sunk and overwhelmed in the waters in the same way. There has been no discrimination. The challenge is to all mankind. Each nation must decide for itself how it will meet it. The choice we make for ourselves must be made with a moderation of counsel and a temperateness of judgment befitting our character and our motives as a nation. We must put excited feeling away. Our motive will not be revenge or the victorious assertion of the physical might of the nation, but only the vindication of right, of human right, of which we are only a single champion. . . .

With a profound sense of the solemn and even tragical character of the step I am taking and of the grave responsibilities which it involves, but in unhesitating obedience to what I deem my constitutional duty, I advise that the Congress declare the recent course of the Imperial German Government to be in fact nothing less than war against the government and people of the United States; that it formally accept the status of belligerent which has thus been thrust upon it; and that it take immediate steps not only to put the country in a more thorough state of defense but also to exert all its power and employ all its resources to bring the Government of the German Empire to terms and end the war.

U.S. Senate. President Woodrow Wilson's War Message to Congress, Senate Doc. 5, 65th Cong., 1st sess., April 2, 1917.

✫ Chapter 2 ✫

The Battle Front

The people who lived through it knew it as the Great War. Only with the outbreak of a second, greater conflict in 1939 was the earlier war called the First World War or World War I. The Great War was the first war to involve most of Europe since the defeat of Napoleon in 1815. When it began, many people thought it would last only a few months. The major powers of Europe greeted the outbreak of war in August 1914 with gusto, and men raced to enlist before the action was over. No one at the time knew that the Great War would last four years, cost more than 8 million lives, and change the nature of warfare forever.

Their enthusiasm was soon shattered by the realities of modern warfare. Advances in weaponry made battles bloodier than ever before. For the average soldier, one of the most dreaded developments was trench warfare. Trench warfare arose because modern machine guns and artillery had made the tactics of pre-

vious wars obsolete. The bullets and shells flying through the air compelled soldiers to burrow into the soil to obtain shelter and survive. Life in the trenches was miserable. Soldiers had to deal with dysentery, rats, and a numbing infection called trench foot that resulted from spending hours on end in waterlogged trenches.

Trench warfare was only one of the new tactics developed in the Great War, however. Artillery—a general term for several types of large-caliber mounted firearms—had been used before 1914, but in World War I commanders began to rely heavily on artillery as a way of routing enemy forces from their trenches. Shell-shock—a mental breakdown caused by heavy exposure to exploding shells from enemy artillery—was a common problem among soldiers. Other hallmarks of modern warfare introduced in World War I include poison gas, flame throwers, and tanks, which the British introduced in 1916.

(Left) World War I saw the introduction of trench warfare. (Above) Heavy artillery was used by both sides to penetrate trench defenses.

loved ones. This chapter provides a glimpse of life on the battle front through their firsthand accounts.

The Shift to Trench Warfare

World War I changed the lives of the people who fought in it. Many soldiers recorded their thoughts and experiences in diaries and in letters to friends and

On September 14, 1914, following a crucial German defeat at the First Battle of the Marne in northeastern France, Prussian minister of war Erich von Falkenhayn stepped in to replace

German corpses decay in northeastern France after the German defeat in the First Battle of the Marne.

Helmuth von Moltke as chief of the German General Staff. In his postwar memoirs, Falkenhayn argued that the shift to trench warfare early in World War I was due to necessity rather than his own decisions. After their defeat at the Battle of the Marne, German forces along the western front lacked the time and manpower to build more traditional fortifications, and they had to resort to using trenches to stop the French advance into Germany.

G.H.Q. [German headquarters] was fully conscious of the disadvantages involved by the transition to trench war. It was cho-sen purely and simply as being the lesser evil.

No progress was made because of the shortage of troops and material. A retirement was not desired because, as the German lines were very thinly held, the gain which might have been obtained by economizing troops through a shortening of the front bore no relation to the certain disadvantages of such a step. They have already been dealt with in another place. Added to this, no positions and dug-outs had been constructed behind the army at that time. It was doubtful whether it would be possible to build them in time in the winter. It was to be assumed that the increase of the front line garrisons [troops] necessitated thereby would use up almost all the troops that were thus economized. In no case would the troops obtain the rest which they needed for the welding of their formations, for training and for re-equipment.

The transition to trench warfare was not effected by the independent decision of the Chief of the General Staff, but under the stern pressure of necessity.

It was very soon realized, however, that this kind of warfare, alternating with hard, well-prepared blows directed against sections of the enemy, was the only means by which it could be hoped to bring the war to a favourable end in view of the change made in the Central Powers' position by the events on the Marne. . . . It was only by its adoption that Germany was able permanently to hold her frontiers [borders]. But the frontiers had to be held, not because G.H.Q. lacked the courage to abandon German soil temporarily to the enemy if the common good had demanded this, but because the loss of the frontier territories would have rendered the continuation of the war impossible after a comparatively short time. The industrial and agricultural districts of the East were quite as important as the industrial districts on both banks of

the Rhine. Neither the exclusion of the one nor the other was practicable for Germany or her allies.

But the transition to trench warfare once more allowed full advantage to be taken of the internal lines and so restored the freedom of action to strike with sufficient forces wherever a decision was necessary.

It was the systematic application of trench warfare which first rendered possible such an increase in the capacity of the railways that they became in effect the

German troops leave for the western front.

equivalent of a reduplication of the reserves.

It was this which first gave time to exploit science and engineering to their full extent in the interests of the war. Thereby it supplied a basis on which brave and well-trained men inferior in number could hold out indefinitely against a manifold superiority.

The first premise, at all events for the successful application of this form of warfare, was the intrinsic superiority of one's own troops over the enemy. That this existed with regard to the Russians was certain. After a short observation, however, the question whether a similar comparison existed with regard to the enemies in the West, who were to be rated more highly, could also be answered with a definite affirmative. Although the German Army, in contrast to the French, for example, had not had a really thorough peace-time training in trench fighting, the troops succeeded in mastering it far more quickly and better than any one of the enemies. Contrary to all expectations, the French, in particular, did not distinguish themselves at all in this. The old truth that the soldier who is well-disciplined and has his heart in the business, and in addition has learnt to attack, is equal to any situation in war, was once more fully confirmed.

Nowhere have the admirable warlike qualities of the German, supplemented by his strict training, celebrated greater triumphs than in the trench war; that is, of the German as he was before the accursed revolution, which was just as unnecessary as it was unfruitful.

Erich von Falkenhayn, *The German General Staff and Its Decisions, 1914–1916*. New York: Dodd, Mead, 1920.

The First Gas Attack

On April 22, 1915, at the start of the Second Battle of Ypres, in northwestern Belgium, the German army under General Erich von Falkenhayn first used chemical gas against French, British, and Canadian forces. British brigadier general J. E. Edmonds describes the surprise, shock, and confusion caused by that first gas attack.

The 22nd April was a glorious spring day. Air reconnaissance [reports from aircraft surveillance] in the morning had disclosed considerable liveliness behind the German lines and some activity in the Houthulst Forest (2 miles north of Langemarck [Belgium]), where a column [long, narrow file of troops] was seen on the march, though it tried to evade observation; but there was nothing abnormal in this. In the forenoon there was considerable shelling of Ypres by 17-inch and 8-inch howitzers and lighter guns, and towards midday, of the roads leading into the town; but this gradually ceased and all was quiet again.

Suddenly, at 5 p.m., a new and furious bombardment of Ypres by heavy howitzers [a type of artillery] was recommenced. The villages in front of Ypres, almost untouched until then, were also heavily shelled, and simultaneously French field-guns to the northeast of Ypres began a somewhat rapid fire, although the German field artillery was silent. At first some officers who heard the firing surmised that the newly arrived Algerian Division [French colonial troops from Morocco and Algeria] was "shooting itself in"; but those who were on points of vantage saw two curious greenish-yellow clouds on the ground on either side of Langemarck in front of the German line. These clouds spread laterally, joined up, and, moving before a light wind, became a bluish-white mist, such as is seen over water meadows on a frosty night. Behind the mist the enemy, by the sound of his rifle fire, was advancing. Soon, even as far off as the V Corps report centre at "Goldfish Chateau" (2,000 yards west of Ypres railway station and five miles from Langemarck) a peculiar smell was noticed, accompanied by smarting of the eyes and tingling of the nose and the throat. It was some little time, however,

German troops emerge from a phosgene cloud. The toxic gas provided cover for the advancing troops and caused injury to the enemy.

before it was realized that the yellow clouds were due to the gas about which warnings had been received, and almost simultaneously French coloured troops, without officers, began drifting down the roads through the back areas of the V Corps. Soon afterwards French Territorial troops were seen hurriedly crossing the bridges over the canal north of Ypres. It was impossible to understand what the Africans said, but from the way they coughed and pointed to their throats, it was evident that, if not suffering from the effects of gas, they were thoroughly scared. Teams and wagons of the French field artillery next appeared retiring, and the throng of fugitives soon became thicker and more disordered, some individuals running and continuing to run until they reached Vlamertinghe [Belgium] and beyond. Although the "seventy-fives" were firing regularly, it was obvious that something very serious had happened, and this was emphasized when, about 7 p.m., the French guns suddenly ceased fire.

Guy Chapman, ed., *Vain Glory: A Miscellany of the Great War 1914–1918; Written by Those Who Fought in It on Each Side and on All Fronts.* London: Cassell, 1968.

A Soldier's Disgust with the War

American novelist John Dos Passos served as an ambulance driver in France and Italy during World War I, and after the war used his wartime diary and letters to write his first novel, One Man's Initiation—1917. *In this August 23, 1917, letter to Rumsey Marvin, a close college friend at Harvard University, Dos Passos voices his disgust and disillusionment with war. He says that the war is being fought only because of disputes between governments, and that there is actually little enmity between Allied and German soldiers.*

Dear Rummy

I've been meaning to write you again & again—but I've been so vastly bitter that I can produce nothing but gall and wormwood [bitterness].

The war is utter damn nonsense—a vast cancer fed by lies and self seeking malignity [harm] on the part of those who don't do the fighting.

Of all the things in this world a government is the thing least worth fighting for.

None of the poor devils whose mangled dirty bodies I take to the hospital in my ambulance really give a damn about any of the aims of this ridiculous affair—They fight because they are too cowardly & too unimaginative not to see which way they ought to turn their guns—

For God's sake, Rummy boy, put this in your pipe and smoke it—everything said & written & thought in America about the war is lies—God! They choke one like poison gas—

I am sitting, my gas mask over my shoulder, my tin helmet on my head—in a poste de secours—(down underground) near a battery of 220s which hit one over the head with their infernal barking as I write.

Apart from the utter bitterness I feel about the whole thing, I've been enjoying

The injured and dying lay on stretchers as French soldiers look on.

my work immensely—We've been for a week in what they say is the hottest sector an ambulance ever worked—All the time—ever since our section of twenty Fiat cars climbed down the long hill into the shot-to-hell valley back of this wood that most of our work is in, we've been under intermittent bombardment.

My first night of work I spent five hours in a poste de secours under poison gas—Of course we had our masks—but I can't imagine a more hellish experience. Every night

we get gassed in this sector—which is right behind the two points where the great advance of the 21st of August was made—look it up & you'll see that we were kept busy—we evacuated from between the two big hills.

It's remarkable how many shells can explode round you without hitting you.

Our ambulance however is simply peppered with holes—how the old bus holds together is more than I can make out—

Do send news of yourself—and think about the war—and don't believe anything people tell you—'ceptin tis me—or anyone else whose really been here.

Incidentally [peace activist] Jane Addams account that the soldiers were fed rum & ether before attacks is true. No human being can stand the performance without constant stimulants—

It's queer how much happier I am here in the midst of it than in America, where the air was stinking with lies & hypocritical patriotic gibber— . . .

In fact there is less bitterness about the war—at the front—than there is over an ordinary Harvard-Yale baseball game.

It's damned remarkable how universally decent people are if you'll only leave them to themselves—

I could write on for hours, but I'm rather sleepy—so I think I'll take a nap among the friendly fleas—

Love

Jack

John Dos Passos, *The Fourteenth Chronicle: Letters and Diaries of John Dos Passos.* Edited and with a biographical narrative by Townsend Ludington. Boston: Gambit, 1973.

The Blind Man

As in any war, many soldiers who fought in World War I suffered horrific injuries. This account by Mary Borden, an American nurse who ran a hospital unit on the western front—the western boundary of Germany along which German and Allied forces clashed—is one example. It is excerpted from Borden's 1929 book, The Forbidden Zone.

It was just before midnight when the stretcher bearers brought in the blind man, and there was no space on the floor anywhere; so they stood waiting, not knowing what to do with him.

I said from the floor in the second row, "Just a minute, old ones. You can put him here in a minute." So they waited with the blind man suspended in the bright, hot misty air between them, like a pair of old horses in shafts with their heads down.

"Put this one in the corridor to make more room here," I said; and I saw them lift him up. When they had taken him away, the stretcher bearers who had been waiting brought the blind one and put him down in the cleared space.

The limbs seemed to be held together only by the strong stuff of the uniform. The head was unrecognizable. It was a monstrous thing, and a dreadful rattling sound came from it. I looked over and saw the chief surgeon standing over me. I don't know how he got there. His small shrunken face was wet and white; his eyes were brilliant and feverish; his incredible hands that saved so many men so exquisitely, so quickly, were in the pockets of his white coat.

"Give him morphine," he said, "a double dose. As much as you like." Then he vanished like a ghost. He went back to the operating room, a small white figure with round shoulders, a magician, who performed miracles with knives.

I gave the morphine, then crawled over and looked at the blind man's ticket. I did not know, of course, that he was blind until I read his ticket. A large round white helmet covered the top half of his head and face; only his nostrils and mouth and chin were uncovered. The surgeon in the dressing station behind the trenches had written on his ticket, "Shot through the eyes. Blind."

Did he know, I asked myself. No, he couldn't know yet. He would still be wondering, waiting, hoping, down there in

A nurse talks to blinded soldiers. Many who survived World War I suffered disfiguring injuries.

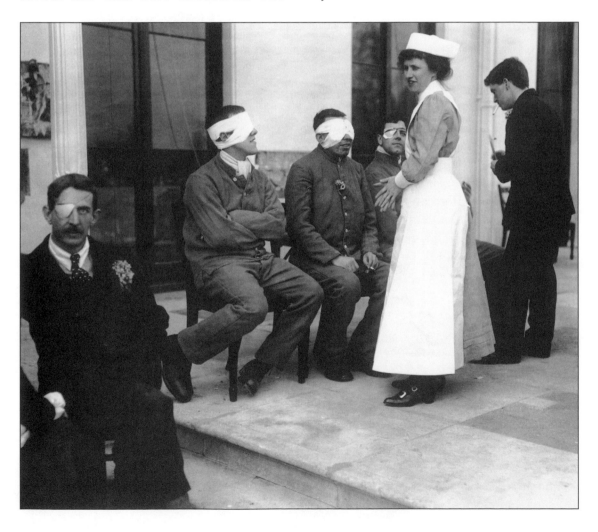

that deep, dark silence of his, in his own dark personal world. He didn't know he was blind; no one would have told him. I felt his pulse. It was strong and steady. He was a long, thin man, but his body was not very cold and the pale lower half of his clear-cut face was not very pale. There was something beautiful about him. In his case there was no hurry, no necessity to rush him through to the operating room. There was plenty of time. He would always be blind.

I said to the blind one, "Here is a drink." He didn't hear me so I said it more loudly against the bandage, and helped him to lift his head, and held the tin cup to his mouth below the thick end of the bandage. The blind man said to me, "Thank you, sister, you are very kind. That is good. I thank you." He had a beautiful voice. I noticed the great courtesy of his speech. But they were all courteous. Their courtesy when they died, their reluctance to cause me any trouble by dying or suffering, was one of the things it didn't do to think about.

Mary Borden, *The Forbidden Zone.* London: W. Heinemann, 1929.

German flying ace Baron Manfred von Richthofen shot down eighty Allied aircraft during World War I.

Memoirs of the Red Baron

The best fighter pilots in World War I were known as flying aces, and none had more successes than German pilot Manfred von Richthofen, who shot down eighty Allied aircraft before being brought down himself by ground fire on April 18, 1918.

Von Richthofen painted his plane red and nicknamed it "the Red Baron." In Great Britain von Richthofen became an object of Allied propaganda, which portrayed him as a man who enjoyed killing.

Von Richthofen's memoirs were published in Germany during the war years, and were subject to the propaganda and censorship prevalent at the time. In this excerpt from the English edition, von Richthofen gloatingly describes his victory over English flying ace Lanoe George Hawker in a November 1916 dogfight, an aerial battle between two planes.

In view of the character of our fight it was clear to me that I had been tackling a flying champion. One day I was blithely flying to give chase when I noticed three Englishmen who also had apparently gone a-hunting. I noticed that they were ogling me and as I felt much inclination to have a fight I did not want to disappoint them.

I was flying at a lower altitude. Consequently I had to wait until one of my English friends tried to drop on me. After a short while one of the three came sailing along and attempted to tackle me in the rear. After firing five shots he had to stop for I had swerved in a sharp curve.

The Englishman tried to catch me up in the rear while I tried to get behind him. So we circled round and round like madmen after one another at an altitude of about 10,000 feet.

First we circled twenty times to the left, and then thirty times to the right. Each tried to get behind and above the other. Soon I discovered that I was not meeting a beginner. He had not the slightest intention of breaking off the fight. He was traveling in a machine [airplane] which turned beautifully. However, my own was better at rising than his, and I succeeded at last in getting above and beyond my English waltzing partner.

When we had got down to about 6,000 feet without having achieved anything in particular, my opponent ought to have discovered that it was time for him to take his leave. The wind was favorable to me for it drove us more and more towards the Ger-

man position. At last we were above Bapaume, about half a mile behind the German front. The impertinent fellow was full of cheek and when we had got down to about 3,000 feet he merrily waved to me as if he would say, "Well, how do you do?"

The circles which we made around one another were so narrow that their diameter was probably no more than 250 or 300 feet. I had time to take a good look at my opponent. I looked down into his carriage and could see every movement of his head. If he had not had his cap on I would have noticed what kind of a face he was making.

My Englishman was a good sportsman, but by and by the thing became a little too hot for him. He had to decide whether he would land on German ground or whether he would fly back to the English lines. Of course he tried the latter, after having endeavored in vain to escape me by loopings and such like tricks. At that time his first bullets were flying around me, for hitherto neither of us had been able to do any shooting.

When he had come down to about three hundred feet he tried to escape by flying in a zig-zag course during which, as is well known, it is difficult for an observer to shoot. That was my most favorable moment. I followed him at an altitude of from two hundred and fifty feet to one hundred and fifty feet, firing all the time. The Englishman could not help falling. But the jamming of my gun nearly robbed me of my success.

My opponent fell, shot through the head, one hundred and fifty feet behind our line. His machine gun was dug out of the ground and it ornaments the entrance of my dwelling.

Manfred von Richthofen, *The Red Air Fighter.* London: The "Aeroplane" & General Publishing Company, 1918.

Americans Take Belleau Wood

The Battle of Belleau Wood, from June 10 to 17, 1918, was one of the first military actions of World War I in which American troops played a major role. In the battle, U.S. Marines ousted German units from a heavily forested wood, helping stop the last major German offensive of the war. As war correspondent Edwin L. James describes in this June 20, 1918, report of the battle, the marines had to take on fortified German machine-gun nests and faced heavy artillery fire. At the end of the battle, the marine brigade had suffered 55 percent casualties: 1,062 killed and 3,615 wounded. Grateful French civilians later renamed the area Bois de la Brigade Marine— "the wood of the Marines."

I believe that when the history of the war is written the Americans' capture of the Bois de Belleau will be ranked among the neatest pieces of military work of the conflict.

Five days ago [June 9], after the capture of the town of Bouresches, the Americans started the task of taking away the Bois de Belleau from the Germans. In the rush at Bouresches they had been unable to secure the rocky strongholds in the woods, and passed on, leaving many nests of machine guns there, which afterward kept up a harassing fire. The Americans several times made big raids into the woods, clearing out part of the Germans, but the next day the Germans would reappear with a harassing fire. Despite strong artillery work, the Germans seemed able to stay there.

On Sunday, the 9th, a rain of extra heavy artillery fire began on the woods. This kept up all Sunday night and Monday. On Monday night the fire was redoubled and the woods literally raked with lines of shellfire.

At about 3 o'clock Monday morning [June 10] the marines started, as soon as the artillery fire was stopped, to go through those woods. At the nearer edge of the woods, devastated by our shellfire, they encountered little opposition. A little further on the Germans made a small stand, but were completely routed; that is, those who were not killed. By this time the marines were fairly started on their way. They swept forward, clearing out machine gun nests with rifle fire, bayonets, and hand grenades.

The Germans started in headlong flight when the Americans seized two machine guns and turned them on the Germans with terrific effect. The Germans soon tired of this, and those nearest the Americans began surrendering. In the meantime, the marines kept up the chase.

While this was going on, the Americans almost rounded the woods, and the Germans, fleeing from some of the Americans, ran into the machine gun and rifle fire of the others. Then those left rushed head-

An American soldier stabs his bayonet into a German soldier in this illustration of the Battle of Belleau Wood.

vision, which includes the Queen Elizabeth Regiment. There had been 1,200 Germans in the woods. With the exception of the prisoners nearly all the rest were slain.

The prisoners said they were glad of the chance to surrender and get out of the woods, because the American artillery fire for three days had cut off their food and other supplies and they had lived in a hell on earth. The Germans seemed deeply impressed by the fury of the American attack. One of the captured officers, when asked what he thought of the Americans as fighters, answered that the artillery was crazy and the infantry drunk. A little German private, taking up his master's thought, pointed to three tousled but smiling marines, and said: "*Vin rouge, vin blanc, beaucoup vin*" [Red wine, white wine, a lot of wine]. He meant he thought the Americans must be intoxicated, to fight as they did for that wood.

Our boys took especial delight in corralling the machine guns. These guns had been very well placed behind trees and in rocky caves and well supplied with ammunition. The Americans had practiced on a German machine gun previously captured, and knew just how to use them against the "Heinies" [Germans]. The captured guns were cleverly camouflaged and were almost overlooked by the Americans. The mortars

long the other way to surrender. In a short time the gallant marines had got to the other side of the woods, and immediately, with the aid of the engineers, started the construction of a strong position.

Prisoners counted that day numbered more than 300. It was found that they belonged to the crack 5th German Guard Dihad been used to throw gas shells from the heights into the woods upon the Americans.

There was the greatest surprise among the American officers at the evident low morale among members of the 5th Guard Division, thought to be one of the Kaiser's very best.

The Germans had tried their best to get the Americans out of the wood and to hold the valuable position. They had sent attack after attack there, always failing to gain complete free possession, but making things very unpleasant for our men. It was after four days of this that the marines got on their hind legs and went after the Germans.

An American General tonight characterized the capture of Belleau Wood as the most important thing the Americans at the front had yet accomplished. Its possession straightens our line, taking away from the German his protected wedge into our positions, and gives an excellent starting point for further operations.

Edwin L. James, *Current History,* June 20, 1918.

Preparing for the Battle of Saint-Mihiel

In this selection from his memoirs, John J. Pershing, commander of the American Expeditionary Force (AEF), explains the magnitude of the logistical challenge facing the American army as it prepared for the Battle of Saint-Mihiel in northeastern France in September 1918. This was the first battle that the AEF executed as an independent unit. (Prior to the Battle of Saint-Mihiel U.S. divisions had fought only in support of French and British units.) Pershing details the work required to move more than half a million men at night by railroad, in trucks, and on foot.

Preparations were being hastened in the hope that the St. Mihiel attack might be made by the 7th of September. Our divisions were scattered and it seemed doubtful whether sufficient rail or truck transportation could be found to bring them in the area, together with the corps and army troops and auxiliaries, before the rainy season, which usually starts about the middle of September and which, it was said, might seriously hinder operations in that sector. It was necessary to assemble in all 550,000 troops for this operation, and this gigantic task, imposed mainly upon the First Army General Staff, which itself was yet in the formative state, might well have caused dismay, even under the most favorable circumstances.

The almost total inactivity on the St. Mihiel front since 1916 made many installations necessary in preparation for an operation of such magnitude. The telephone and telegraph lines, to insure effective communication throughout the area, needed many miles of wire. Artillery ammunition, calculated on the basis of at least five days of battle, was necessary in the amount of about 3,300,000 rounds. Engineering material for building roads across no-man's-land behind the advancing army ran into thousands of tons. Rail-

Soldiers from the Eighteenth Infantry Machine Gun Battalion pass through the ruins of war on their way to the Battle of Saint-Mihiel.

way spurs, advance depots, and hospital accommodations for sick and wounded had to be provided and aviation fields prepared. Many other things were required, such as the construction of light railways for distribution beyond the railheads, personnel and equipment pertaining to searchlights, the development of water supply, installations for sound and flash ranging for artillery, arrangements for traffic control and the camouflage of positions, roads and material. Each item was the subject of consideration by qualified specialists and all had to be coordinated by the newly formed staff.

The actual movement for the concentration of the more than one-half million men, whether by rail, truck, or on foot, generally took place at night. The troops bivouacked [camped] during the day in forests or other sheltered places hidden from the observation of enemy airplanes, resuming the movement at nightfall. The rail and most of the truck transport belonged to the French and was handled by them. Changes were constantly necessary in schedules on account of the nonarrival of trucks as planned, usually due to their being used elsewhere by the French.

All ranks of the staff and line were filled with enthusiasm at the prospect of the coming operation. Officers of the rapidly expanding First Army Staff worked with the greatest energy under their new responsibilities. The French officers assigned to my headquarters gave material assistance in expediting the arrival of French troops and in handling the civilian population within the Zone of the Armies. These officers were deeply interested and the spirit of cooperation between French and Americans in the untiring efforts given to preparation foretold the favorable outcome of our first offensive.

John J. Pershing, *My Experiences in the First World War.* New York: Frederick A. Stokes, 1931.

An American Flying Ace at the Battle of Saint-Mihiel

The most successful American flying ace was Eddie Rickenbacker, who had a recorded twenty-six kills. In 1919 Rickenbacker wrote an autobiography entitled Fighting the Flying Circus, *in reference to the German fighter group known for the bright colors of its planes. In this excerpt, Rickenbacker describes his role in the September 1918 Battle of Saint-Mihiel.*

At dinner that night—the night of my arrival word came to us that the Big Show [the battle] was to start at five o'clock the following morning.

Precisely at five o'clock I was awakened by the thundering of thousands of colossal guns. It was September 12, 1918. The St. Mihiel Drive was on!

Leaping out of bed I put my head outside the tent. We had received orders to be over the lines at daybreak in large formations. It was an exciting moment in my life as I realized that the great American attack upon which so many hopes had been fastened was actually on. I suppose every American in the world wanted to be in that great attack. The very sound of the guns thrilled one and filled one with excitement. The good reputation of America seemed bound up in the outcome of that attack.

Dressing with great haste I ran over through the rain to the mess hall. There I found groups of the fellows all standing about impatiently awaiting the chance to get away. But the weather was certainly too bad to attempt any flight to the lines. We were compelled to wait until daylight to see the true state of the heavens.

About noon word came to us that the attack was progressing quite favorably. None of our machines had been able to get up. It was still raining but the visibility was getting better. We could see that the clouds were nearly a thousand feet above the ground.

Taking Reed Chambers one side, I proposed to him that despite the rain we try a short flip over the lines to see for ourselves what it was like. He agreed and while the others were at lunch we climbed into our machines and made off. At 60 feet above ground we found that we were just under the clouds and still had quite a long view of the landscape.

Flying straight east to St. Mihiel, we crossed the Meuse River and turned down its valley towards Verdun. Many fires were burning under us as we flew, most of them well on the German side of the river. Villages, haystacks, ammunition dumps and supplies were being set ablaze by the retreating Huns [Germans].

We proceeded as far as Verdun. Then turning east we continued flying at our low altitude and passed over Fresnes and Vigneulles.

Vigneulles was the objective point of the American forces. It lies east of Verdun some fifteen miles and about the same distance north of St. Mihiel. One American army was pushing towards it from a point just south of Verdun while the other attack was made from the opposite side of the salient [an outwardly projecting piece of land]. Like irresistible pincers, the two forces were drawing nearer and nearer to

Eddie Rickenbacker, credited with twenty-six kills during World War I, proved the most successful American flying ace of the war.

this objective point. The German troops who were still inside the salient would soon be caught inside the pincers.

As Reed and I turned south from Vigneulles we saw that the main highway running north to Metz was black with hurrying men and vehicles. Guns, stores and ammunition were being hauled away to safety with all possible speed. We continued on south through the very heart of the St. Mihiel salient, flying always low above the roadway which connected Vigneulles with St. Mihiel. Here, likewise, we found the Germans in full cry to the rear.

One especially attractive target presented itself to us as we flew along this road. A whole battery of Boche three-inch guns [a type of artillery] was coming towards us on the double. They covered fully half a mile of the roadway.

Dipping down at the head of the column I sprinkled a few bullets over the leading teams. Horses fell right and left. One driver leaped from his seat and started running for the ditch. Half-way across the road he threw up his arms and rolled over, upon his face. He had stepped full in front of my stream of machine-gun bullets!

All down the line we continued our fire—now tilting our aeroplanes down for a short burst, then zooming back up for a little altitude in which to repeat the performance. The whole column was thrown into the wildest confusion. Horses plunged and broke away. Some were killed and fell in their tracks. Most of the drivers and gunners had taken to the trees before we reached them. Our little visit must have cost them an hour's delay.

Passing over St. Mihiel, we hastened on to our aerodrome [air base]. There we immediately telephoned headquarters information of what we had seen and particularly of the last column of artillery we had shot up in its retreat from St. Mihiel. This was evidently splendid news and exactly what GHQ [general headquarters] had been anxious to know, for they questioned us closely upon this subject, inquiring whether or not we were convinced that the Germans were actually quitting St. Mihiel.

Eddie Rickenbacker, *Fighting the Flying Circus.* New York: Frederick A. Stokes, 1919.

A German Officer at the Meusse-Argonne Offensive

The Meusse-Argonne offensive began on October 18, 1918, and lasted until the end of the war on November 11. American general John J. Pershing was given overall command of the operation, and the American Expeditionary Force took on the main attacking role. During the offensive, particularly fierce fighting occurred between American and German forces in the heights of the Romagne Forest, Cunel, and the eastern edge of the Argonne Forest. In this excerpt from his published diary Storm of Steel, *former German soldier Ernst Junger describes a devastating attack on his company.*

Everybody had that clutching feeling: 'It's coming over!' There was a terrific stupefying crash . . . the shell had burst in the midst of us. . . .

I picked myself up half-conscious. The machine-gun ammunition in the large shell-hole, set alight by the explosion, was burning an intense pink glow. It illumined the rising fumes of the shell-burst, in which there writhed a heap of black bodies and the shadowy forms of the survivors, who were rushing from the scene in all directions. At the same time rose a multitudinous tumult of pain and cries for help.

I will make no secret of it that after a moment's blank horror I took to my heels like the rest and ran aimlessly into the night. It was not till I had fallen head over heels into a small shell-hole that I understood what had happened. Only to hear and see no more! Only to get away, far away, and creep into a hole! And yet the other voice was heard: 'You are the company commander, man!' Exactly so. I do not say it in self-praise. . . . I have often observed in myself and others that an officer's sense of responsibility drowns his personal fears. There is a sticking-place, something to occupy the thoughts. So I forced myself back to the ghastly spot. . . .

The wounded men never ceased to utter their fearful cries. Some came creeping to me when they heard my voice and whimpered, 'Sir . . . Sir!' One of my favourite recruits, Jasinski, whose leg was broken . . . , caught hold of me round the knees. Cursing my impotence to help, I vainly clapped him on the shoulder. Such moments can never be forgotten.

the thousands that passed the slightest difference. All moved under a cloak of invisibility. Only after the most numerous and severe tests at all distances, with all materials and combinations of colors that give forth no color could this gray have been discovered. That it was selected to clothe and disguise the German when he fights is typical of the German staff striving for efficiency to leave nothing to chance, to neglect no detail.

After you have seen this service uniform under conditions entirely opposite you are convinced that for the German soldier it is his strongest weapon. Even the most expert marksman cannot hit a target he cannot see. It is a gray green, not the blue gray of our Confederates. It is the gray of the hour just before daybreak, the gray of unpolished steel, of mist among green trees.

I saw it first in the Grand Place in front of the Hotel de Ville. It was impossible to tell if in that noble square there was a regiment or a brigade. You saw only a fog that melted into the stones, blended with the ancient house fronts, that shifted and drifted, but left you nothing at which you could point.

Later, as the army passed below my window, under the trees of the Botanical Park, it merged and was lost against the green leaves. It is no exaggeration to say that at a hundred yards you can see the horses on which the Uhlans ride, but cannot see the men who ride them.

If I appear to overemphasize this disguising uniform it is because of all the details of the German outfit, it appealed to me as one of the most remarkable. The other day, when I was with the rear guard of the French Dragoons and Curassiers [types of soldiers] and they threw out pickets, we could distinguish them against the yellow wheat or green course at half a mile, while these men passing in the street, when they have reached the next crossing, become merged into the gray of the paving stones and the earth swallows them. . . .

Yesterday Major General von Jarotzky, the German Military Governor of Brussels, assured Burgomaster Max that the German army would not occupy the city, but would pass through it. It is still passing. I have followed in campaigns six armies, but, excepting not even our own, the Japanese or the British, I have not seen one so thoroughly equipped. I am not speaking of the fighting qualities of any army, only of the equipment and organization. The German army moved into this city as smoothly and as compactly as an Empire State Express [an American train]. There were not halts, no open places, no stragglers.

This army has been on active service three weeks, and so far there is not apparently a chinstrap or a horseshoe missing. It came in with the smoke pouring from cookstoves on wheels, and in an hour had set up postoffice wagons, from which mounted messengers galloped along the line of column distributing letters and at which soldiers posted picture postcards.

The infantry came in in files of five, two hundred men to each company; the Lances in columns of four, with not a pennant [flag] missing. The quick fire guns and field

German troops exhibit a powerful presence as they march in unison.

pieces were one hour at a time in passing, each gun with its caisson and ammunition wagon taking twenty seconds in which to pass.

The men of the infantry sang "Fatherland, My Fatherland." Between each line of song they took three steps. At times two thousand men were singing together in absolute rhythm and beat. When the melody gave way the silence was broken only by the stamp of iron-shod boots, and then again the song rose. When the singing ceased the bands played marches. They were followed by the rumble of siege guns, the creaking of wheels and of chains clanking against the cobble stones and the sharp bell-like voices of the bugles.

For seven hours the army passed in such solid column that not once might a taxicab or trolley car pass through the city. Like a river of steel it flowed, gray and ghostlike. Then, as dusk came and as thousands of horses' hoofs and thousands of iron boots continued to tramp forward, they struck tiny sparks from the stones, but the horses and the men who beat out the sparks were invisible.

At midnight pack wagons and siege guns were still passing. At 7 this morning I was awakened by the tramp of men and bands playing jauntily. Whether they marched all night or not I do not know; but now for twenty-six hours the gray army has rumbled by with the mystery of fog and the pertinacity of a steam roller.

Richard Harding Davis, *New York Tribune*, August 23, 1914.

Over There

In 1917, American writers such as Broadway star George M. Cohan joined the war effort by composing patriotic songs in support of U.S. troops. By the time the United States entered the war, Cohan had produced and starred in numerous hit musicals, featuring such songs as "The Yankee Doodle Dandy" and "Give My Regards to Broadway." Ultimately, "Over There" became his most famous song.

American soldiers line the upper decks of a transport ship.

Johnnie get your gun, get your gun, get
    your gun,
Take it on the run, on the run, on the run;
Hear them calling you and me;
Every son of liberty.
Hurry right away, no delay, go today,
Make your daddy glad, to have had such a
    lad,
Tell your sweetheart not to pine,
To be proud of her boy's in line.

Chorus:
Over there, over there,
Send the word, send the word over
    there,
That the Yanks are coming, the Yanks are
    coming,
The drums rum-tumming everywhere.
So prepare, say a prayer,
Send the word, send the word to beware,
We'll be over, we're coming over,
And we won't come back till it's over over
    there.

Johnnie get your gun, get your gun, get
    your gun,
Johnnie show the Hun, you're a son-of-a-
    gun,
Hoist the flag and let her fly,
Like true heroes do or die.
Pack your little kit, show your grit, do your
    bit,
Soldiers to the ranks from the towns and
    the tanks,
Make your mother proud of you,
And to liberty be true.

George M. Cohan, "Over There," 1917.

"Not Our War"

Radical journalist John Reed, an editor of the socialist magazine Masses, *criticized the U.S. intervention in World War I in the April 1917 issue of that magazine. He denounced the war as a "rich man's war and a poor man's fight," implying that the war would benefit wealthy financiers (whose banks made loans to the Allies) and industrialists (who owned the factories that produced war supplies for the Allies) at the expense of average workers. Reed also argues that the United States had favored the Allies since the beginning of the war, even though England, France, and Russia engaged in acts that were just as deplorable as Germany's submarine warfare.*

I know what war means. I have been with the armies of all the belligerents except one, and I have seen men die, and go mad, and lie in hospitals suffering hell; but there is a worse thing than that. War means an ugly mob-madness, crucifying the truth-tellers, choking the artists, sidetracking reforms, revolutions, and the working of social forces. Already in America those citizens who oppose the entrance of their country into the European melee are called "traitors," and those who protest against the curtailing of our meagre rights of free speech are spoken of as "dangerous lunatics." We have had a forecast of the censorship—when the naval authorities . . . cut off American news from Germany, and only the wildest fictions reached Berlin via London, creating a perilous situation. . . . The press is howling for war. The church is howling for war. Lawyers, politicians, stock-brokers, social leaders are all howling for war. Roosevelt is again recruiting his thrice-thwarted family regiment.

But whether it comes to actual hostilities or not, some damage has been done. The militarists have proved their point. I know of at least two valuable social movements that have suspended functioning because no one cares. For many years this country is going to be a worse place for free men to live in; less tolerant, less hos-

pitable. Maybe it is too late, but I want to put down what I think about it all.

A War for the Rich

Whose war is this? Not mine. I know that hundreds of thousands of American workingmen employed by our great financial "patriots" are not paid a living wage. I have seen poor men sent to jail for long terms without trial, and even

Workers toil in an American munitions factory during World War I.

without any charge. Peaceful strikers, and their wives and children, have been shot to death, burned to death, by private detectives and militiamen. The rich have steadily become richer, and the cost of living higher, and the workers proportionally poorer. These toilers don't want war—not even civil war. But the speculators, the employers, the plutocracy [the wealthy and powerful]—they want it, just as they did in Germany and in England; and with lies and sophistries they will whip up our blood until we are savage—and then we'll fight and die for them.

I am one of a vast number of ordinary people who read the daily papers, and occasionally [the Democratic magazine] *The New Republic*, and want to be fair. We don't know much about international politics; but we want our country to keep off the necks of little nations, to refuse to back up American beasts of prey who invest abroad and get their fingers burned, and to stay out of quarrels not our own. We've got an idea that international law is the crystallized common-sense of nations, distilled from their experiences with each other, and that it holds good for all of them, and can be understood by anybody.

We are simple folk. Prussian militarism seemed to us insufferable; we thought the invasion of Belgium a crime; German atrocities horrified us, and also the idea of German submarines exploding ships full of peaceful people without warning. But then we began to hear about England and France jailing, fining, exiling and even

shooting men who refused to go out and kill; the Allied armies invaded and seized a part of neutral Greece, and a French admiral forced upon her an ultimatum as shameful as Austria's to Serbia; Russian atrocities were shown to be more dreadful than German; and hidden mines sown by England in the open sea exploded ships full of peaceful people without warning.

Other things disturbed us. For instance, why was it a violation of international law for the Germans to establish a "war-zone" around the British Isles, and perfectly legal for England to close the North Sea? Why is it we submitted to the British order forbidding the shipment of non-contraband to Germany, and insisted upon our right to ship contraband to the Allies? If our "national honor" was smirched by Germany's refusal to allow war materials to be shipped to the Allies, what happened to our national honor when England refused to let us ship non-contraband food and even Red Cross hospital supplies to Germany? Why is England allowed to attempt the avowed starvation of German civilians, in violation of international law, when the Germans cannot attempt the same thing without our horrified protest? How is it that the British can arbitrarily regulate our commerce with neutral nations, while we raise a howl whenever the Germans "threaten to restrict our merchant ships going about their business?" Why does our government insist that Americans should not be molested while traveling on Allied ships armed against submarines?

The United States Has Not Truly Been Neutral

American Red Cross workers bring much needed food to orphaned French children.

We have shipped and are shipping vast quantities of war materials to the Allies, we have floated the Allied loans. We have been strictly neutral toward the Teutonic [German and Austro-Hungarian] powers only. Hence the inevitable desperation of the last German note. Hence this war we are on the brink of.

Those of us who voted for Woodrow Wilson did so because we felt his mind and his eyes were open, because he had kept us out of the mad-dog-fight of Europe, and because the plutocracy opposed him. We had learned enough about the war to lose some of our illusions, and we wanted to be neutral. We grant that the President, considering the position he'd got himself into, couldn't do anything else but answer the German note as he did—but if we had been neutral, that note wouldn't have been sent. The President didn't ask us; he won't ask us if we want war or not. The fault is not ours. It is not our war.

John Reed, *Masses*, April 1917.

Strengthening the War Effort Through Propaganda

During World War I, governments often used propaganda—selected information, exaggerations, and sometimes lies—to promote their point of view. In the United States, the federal Committee on Public Information (CPI) used propaganda to bolster support for the war effort. The following excerpts are from a CPI pamphlet distributed to the Boy Scouts of America. In it, the government encourages scouts to help spread the "truth" about the war.

To the Members of the Boy Scouts of America!

Attention, Scouts! We are again called upon to do active service for our country! Every one of the 285,661 Scouts and 76,957 Scout Officials has been summoned by President Woodrow Wilson, Commander-in-Chief of the Army and Navy, to serve as a dispatch bearer from the Government at Washington to the American people all over the country. The prompt, enthusiastic, and hearty response of every one of us has been pledged by our [Scout] President, Mr. Livingstone. Our splendid record of accomplishments in war activities promises full success in this new job.

This patriotic service will be rendered under the slogan: "EVERY SCOUT TO BOOST AMERICA" AS A GOVERNMENT DISPATCH BEARER. The World War is for liberty and democracy. . . .

As a democracy, our country faces great danger—not so much from submarines, battleships and armies, because, thanks to our allies, our enemies have apparently little chance of reaching our shores.

Our danger is from within. Our enemies have representatives everywhere; they tell lies; they misrepresent the truth; they deceive our own people; they are a real menace to our country.

Already we have seen how poor Russia has been made to suffer because her people do not know the truth. Representatives of the enemy have been very effective in their deceitful efforts to make trouble for the [Russian] Government.

Fortunately here in America our people are better educated—they want the truth. Our President recognized the justice and wisdom of this demand when in the early stages of the war he created the Committee on Public Information. He knew that the Government would need the confidence, enthusiasm and willing service of every man and woman, every boy and girl in the nation. He knew that the only possible way to create a genuine feeling of partnership between the people and its representatives in Washington was to take the people into his confidence by full, frank statements concerning the reasons for our entering the war, the various steps taken during the war and the ultimate aims of the war.

Neither the President as Commander-in-Chief, nor our army and navy by land and sea, can alone win the war. At this moment the best defense that America has is an enlightened and loyal citizenship. . . .

Here is where our service begins. We are to help spread the facts about America and America's part in the World War. We are to fight lies with truth.

We are to help create public opinion "just as effective in helping to bring victory as ships and guns," to stir patriotism, the great force behind the ships and guns. Isn't that a challenge for every loyal Scout? . . .

Under the direction of our leaders, the Boy Scouts of America are to serve as an intelligence division of the citizens' army, always prepared and alert to respond to any call which may come from the President of the United States and the Committee on Public Information in Washington.

Committee on Public Information, Boy Scouts of America pamphlet, 1917. Available online at http://longman.awl.com/history/primarysource_22_1.htm (accessed April 11, 2001).

The U.S. government enlisted the aid of organizations such as the Boy Scouts.

The Espionage and Sedition Acts

The Espionage Act, passed by Congress on June 15, 1917, prescribed a $10,000 fine and twenty years' imprisonment for anyone found guilty of aiding enemies of the United States, obstructing military recruitment, or causing insubordination, *disloyalty, or a refusal to serve in the armed forces. The act, criticized as unconstitutional, was used to arrest and imprison many members of the anti-war movement.*

On May 16, 1918, Congress broadened the Espionage Act with the addition of an amendment that made it a crime to "utter, print, write, or publish any disloyal, profane, scurrilous [derisive] or abusive language" about the U.S. government or to "by word or act support or favor the cause of any country with which the United States is at war or by word or act to oppose the cause of the United States." The revised law was known as the Sedition Act.

The Espionage Act

Be it enacted, That section three of the Act . . . approved June 15, 1917, be . . . amended so as to read as follows:

SEC. 3. Whoever, when the United States is at war, shall willfully make or convey false reports or false statements with intent to interfere with the operation or success of the military or naval forces of the United States, or to promote the success of its enemies, or shall willfully make or convey false reports, or false statements, or say or do anything except by way of bona fide and not disloyal advice to an investor . . . with intent to obstruct the sale by the United States of bonds . . . or the making of loans by or to the United States, or whoever, when the United States is at war, shall willfully cause . . . or incite . . . insubordination, disloyalty, mutiny, or refusal of duty, in the military or naval forces of the United States, or shall willfully obstruct . . . the recruiting or enlistment service of the United States, and whoever, when the United States is at war, shall willfully utter, print, write, or publish any disloyal, profane, scurrilous, or abusive language about the form of government of the United States, or the Constitution of the United States, or the military or naval forces of the United States, or the flag . . . or the uniform of the Army or Navy of the United States, or any language intended to bring the form of government . . . or the Constitution . . . or the military or naval forces . . . or the flag . . . of the United States into contempt, scorn, contumely, or disrepute . . . or shall willfully display the flag of any foreign enemy, or shall willfully . . . urge, incite, or advocate any curtailment of production in this country of any thing or things . . . necessary or essential to the prosecution of the war . . . and whoever shall willfully advocate, teach, defend, or suggest the doing of any of the acts or things in this section enumerated and whoever shall by word or act support or favor the cause of any country with which the United States is at war or by word or act oppose the cause of the United States therein, shall be punished by a fine of not more than $10,000 or imprisonment for not more than twenty years, or both.

The Sedition Act

Be it enacted by the Senate and House of Representatives of the United States of America in Congress assembled, that section three of title one of the Act entitled, "An Act to punish acts of interference with the foreign relations, the neutrality, and the foreign commerce of the United States, to punish espionage, and better to enforce the criminal laws of the United States, and for other purposes," approved June fifteenth, nineteen hundred and seventeen, be, and the same is hereby, amended so as to read as follows:

"Sec. 3. Whoever, when the United States is at war, shall willfully make or convey false reports or false statements with intent to interfere with the operation or success of the military or naval forces of the United States, or to promote the success of its enemies, or shall willfully make or convey false reports or false statements, or say or do anything except by way of bona fide and not disloyal advice to an investor or investors, with intent to obstruct the sale by the United States of bonds or other securities of the United States or the making of loans by or to the United States, and whoever, when the United States is at war, shall willfully cause or attempt to cause, or incite or attempt to incite, insubordination, disloyalty, mutiny, or refusal of duty, in the military or naval forces of the United States, or shall willfully obstruct or attempt to obstruct the recruiting or enlistment service of the United States, and whoever, when the United States is at war, shall willfully utter, print, write, or publish any disloyal, profane, scurrilous, or abusive language about the form of government of the United States, or the Constitution of the United States, or the military or naval forces of the United States, or the flag of the United States, or the uniform of the Army or Navy of the United States, or any language intended to bring the form of government of the United States, or the Constitution of the United States, or the military or naval forces of the United States, or the flag of the United States, or the uniform of the Army or Navy of the United States into contempt, scorn, contumely, or disrepute, or shall willfully utter, print, write, or publish any language intended to incite, provoke, or encourage resistance to the United States, or to promote the cause of its enemies, or shall willfully display the flag of any foreign enemy, or shall willfully by utterance, writing, printing, publication, or language spoken, urge, incite, or advocate any curtailment of production in this country of any thing or things, product or products, necessary or essential to the prosecution of the war in which the United States may be engaged, with intent by such curtailment to cripple or hinder the United States in the prosecution of the war, and whoever shall willfully advocate, teach, defend, or suggest the doing of any of the acts or things in this section enumerated, and whoever shall by word or act support or favor the cause of any country with which the United States is at war or by word or act oppose the cause of the United States therein, shall be punished by a fine of not more than $10,000 or imprisonment for not more than twenty years, or both. . . .

Title XII of the said Act of June fifteenth, nineteen hundred and seventeen, be, and the same is hereby, amended by adding thereto the following section:

"Sec. 4. When the United States is at war, the Postmaster General may, upon evidence satisfactory to him that any person or concern is using the mails in violation of any of the provisions of this Act, instruct the postmaster at any post office at which mail is received addressed to such person or concern to return to the postmaster at the office at which they were originally mailed all letters or other matter so addressed, with the words 'Mail to this address undeliverable under Espionage Act' plainly written or stamped upon the outside thereof, and all such letters or other matter so returned to such postmasters shall be by them returned to the senders thereof under such regulations as the Postmaster General may prescribe."

The Espionage Act, June 16, 1917; The Sedition Act, May 16, 1918.

A Socialist Leader Criticizes the War

The first decades of the twentieth century saw the rise of big business. As wealth became increasingly concentrated in the hands of the upper class, a socialist movement emerged to promote reform. The Socialist Party of America pushed for workers' compensation laws, publicly owned utilities for gas, water, and electricity, and social-welfare reforms to alleviate the costs of industrialism.

In 1910 the first Socialist was elected to Congress. In 1912, the party nominated Eugene V. Debs as its candidate for president. Debs lost to Woodrow Wilson, but continued to campaign for labor rights and other causes. In early 1918, encouraged by the late 1917 Bolshevik revolution in Russia, Debs went on the road to speak out against American participation in the war. He knew he would be arrested and prosecuted for criticizing U.S. intervention, but he delivered a number of talks during the first two weeks of June 1918. His remarks before more than one thousand people attending the state convention of the Ohio Socialist Party in Canton, Ohio, are excerpted below. Debs emphasizes the socialist view that the war is fought by members of the working class, but only benefits the wealthy ruling class.

When the Bolsheviki [Russian revolutionaries] came into power and went through the archives they found and exposed the secret treaties—the treaties that were made between the Czar and the French Government, the British Government and the Italian Government, proposing, after the victory was achieved, to dismember the German Empire and destroy the Central Powers. These treaties have never been denied nor repudiated [rejected]. Very little has been said about them in the American press. I have a copy of these treaties, showing that the purpose of the Allies is exactly the purpose of the Central Powers, and that is the conquest and spoliation of the weaker nations that has always been the purpose of war. . . .

The master class has always declared the wars; the subject class has always fought the battles. The master class has had all to gain and nothing to lose, while the subject class has had nothing to gain and all to lose—especially their lives. . . .

The first Socialist elected to congress, Eugene V. Debs, spoke out against the war.

sacrifices, the working class who freely shed their blood and furnish the corpses, have never yet had a voice in either declaring war or making peace. It is the ruling class that invariably does both. They alone declare war and they alone make peace. . . .

What a compliment it is to the Socialist movement to be persecuted for the sake of the truth! The truth alone will make the people free. And for this reason the truth must not be permitted to reach the people. The truth has always been dangerous to the rule of the rogue, the exploiter, the robber. So the truth must be ruthlessly suppressed. That is why they are trying to destroy the Socialist movement; and every time they strike a blow they add a thousand new voices to the hosts proclaiming that Socialism is the hope of humanity. . . .

Do not worry over the charge of treason to your masters, but be concerned about the treason that involves yourselves. Be true to yourself and you cannot be a traitor to any good cause on earth.

Yes, in good time we are going to sweep into power in this nation and throughout the world. We are going to destroy all enslaving and degrading capitalist institutions and recreate them as free and humanizing institutions. The world is daily changing before our eyes. The sun of capitalism is setting; the sun of Socialism is rising. It is our duty to build the new nation

And here let me emphasize the fact— and it cannot be repeated too often—that the working class who fight all the battles, the working class who make the supreme and the free republic. We need industrial and social builders. We Socialists are the builders of the beautiful world that is to be. We are all pledged to do our part. We are inviting—aye challenging you in the name of your own manhood and womanhood to join us and do your part.

In due time the hour will strike and this great cause triumphant—the greatest in history—will proclaim the emancipation of the working class and the brotherhood of all mankind.

Eugene V. Debs, remarks at the Ohio Socialist Party state convention, Canton, Ohio, June 16, 1918.

An African American's View of the War

Most of the black Americans who served in World War I worked as cooks, orderlies, and truck drivers. Those who did serve as combat soldiers were part of black regiments that usually had white officers and were completely segregated from white units.

The Germans, aware of how black Americans were treated in the United States, attempted to persuade them to change sides. Propaganda leaflets recounted the number of blacks who had been lynched in the United States while others fought in Europe. Despite these efforts, no black soldiers deserted in World War I, but in part because of the German tactics, home front protests against lynchings drew suspicion from the government.

In this July 1918 excerpt from his magazine Messenger, *black civil rights advocate Asa Philip Randolph describes a meeting of the Na-tional Association for the Advancement of Colored People (NAACP) in which a government representative warned those assembled that they were suspected of being German sympathizers. Randolph writes that there is little connection between black discontent and "Germanism," or German views and ideology. Randolph was later arrested under the Sedition Act.*

At a recent convention of the National Association for the Advancement of Colored People (NAACP), a member of the Administration's Department of Intelligence was present. When Mr. Julian Carter of Harrisburg was complaining of the racial prejudice which American white troops had carried into France, the administration representative rose and warned the audience that the Negroes were under suspicion of having been affected by German propaganda.

In keeping with the ultra-patriotism of the oldline type of Negro leaders the NAACP failed to grasp its opportunity. It might have informed the Administration representatives that the discontent among Negroes was not produced by propaganda, nor can it be removed by propaganda. The causes are deep and dark—though obvious to all who care to use their mental eyes. Peonage [servitude], disfranchisement [deprivation of rights], Jim-Crowism [laws that enforce racial segregation and discrimination], segregation, rank civil discrimination, injustice of legislatures, courts and administrators—these are the propaganda of discontent among Negroes.

The Fifteenth Regimental Infantry in France, one of the all-black regiments that served in combat.

The only legitimate connection between this unrest and Germanism is the extensive government advertisement that we [the United States] are fighting "to make the world safe for democracy", to carry democracy to Germany; that we are conscripting the Negro into the military and industrial establishments to achieve this end for white democracy four thousand miles away, while the Negro at home, through bearing the burden in every way, is denied economic, political, educational and civil democracy.

Asa Philip Randolph, *Messenger*, July 1918.

The War's Effect on Women

Helen Swanwick was an activist for women's political and economic rights. In this excerpt from her book War in Its Effect upon Women, *Swanwick suggests that the experiences of men and women during wartime are quite different. Writing during the war, she realized that the war on the home front would change the prescribed gender roles for women, leading them to do "men's work"—such as holding full-time jobs.*

How has the war affected women? How will it affect them? Women, as half the human race, are compelled to take their share of evil and good with men, the other half. The destruction of property, the increase of taxation, the rise of prices, the devastation of beautiful things in nature and art—these are felt by men as well as by women. Some losses doubtless appeal to one or the other sex with peculiar poignancy, but it would be difficult to say whose sufferings are the greater, though there can be no doubt at all that men get an exhilaration out of war which is denied to most women. When they see pictures of soldiers encamped in the ruins of what was once a home, amidst the dead bodies of gentle milch cows, most women would be thinking too insistently of the babies who must die for need of milk to entertain the exhilaration which no doubt may be felt at "the good work of our guns." When they read of miles upon miles of kindly earth made barren, the hearts of men may be wrung to think of wasted toil, but to women the thought suggests a simile full of an even deeper pathos [evoking pity or compassion]; they will think of the millions of young lives destroyed, each one having cost the travail and care of a mother, and of the millions of young bodies made barren by the premature death of those who should have been their mates. The millions of widowed maidens in the coming generation will have to turn their thoughts away from one particular joy and fulfilment of life. While men in war give what is, at the present stage of the world's development, the peculiar service of men, let them not forget that in rendering that very service they are depriving a corresponding number of women of the opportunity of rendering what must, at all stages of the world's development, be the peculiar service of women. After the war, men will go on doing what has been regarded as men's work; women, deprived of their own, will also have to do much of what has been regarded as men's work. These things are going to affect women profoundly, and one hopes that the reconstruction of society is going to be met by the whole people—men and women—with a sympathetic understanding of each other's circumstances. When what are known as men's questions are discussed, it is generally assumed that the settlement of them depends upon men only; when what are known as women's questions are discussed, there is never any suggestion that they can be settled by women independently of men. Of course they cannot. But, then, neither can "men's questions" be rightly settled so. In fact, life would be far more truly envisaged [envisioned] if we dropped the silly phrases "men's and women's questions"; for, indeed, there are no such matters, and all human questions affect all humanity.

Now, for the right consideration of human questions, it is necessary for humans to understand each other. This catastrophic war will do one good thing if it opens our eyes to real live women as they are, as we know them in workaday life, but as the politician and the journalist seem not to have known them. When war broke out, a Labour newspaper, in the midst of the news of men's activities, found space to say that women would feel the pinch, because their supply of attar of roses [rose oil] would be curtailed. It struck some women like a blow in the face. When a great naval engagement took place, the front page of a progressive daily was taken up with portraits of the officers and men who had won distinction, and the back page with portraits of simpering mannequins in extravagantly fashionable hats; not frank advertisement, mind you, but exploitation of women under the guise of news supposed to be peculiarly interesting to the feeble-minded creatures. When a snapshot was published of the first women ticket collectors in England, the legend underneath the picture ran "Superwomen"! It took the life and death of Edith Cavell to open the eyes of the Prime Minister to the fact that there were thousands of women giving life and service to their country. "A year ago we did not know it," he said, in the House of Commons [part of the British legislature]. Is that indeed so? Surely in our private capacities as ordinary citizens, we knew not only of the women whose portraits are in the picture papers (mostly pretty ladies of the music hall or of society), but also of the toiling millions upon whose courage and ability and endurance and goodness of heart the great human family rests. Only the politicians did not know, because their thoughts were too much engrossed with faction fights to think humanly; only the journalists would not write of them, because there was more money in writing the columns which are demanded by the advertisers of feminine luxuries. Anyone who has conducted a woman's paper knows the steady commercial pressure for that sort of "copy" [writing, story].

The other kind of women are, through the war, becoming good "copy." But women have not suddenly become patriotic, or capable, or self-sacrificing; the great masses of women have always shown these qualities in their humble daily life. Now that their services are asked for in unfamiliar directions, attention is being attracted to them, and many more people are realising that, with extended training and opportunity, women's capacity for beneficent [beneficial] work would be extended.

Helena Swanwick, *War in Its Effect upon Women*. New York: Garland, 1971.

Chapter 4

The Aftermath

"War-weary" is the term that best describes the mood in the United States, and much of the rest of the world, in 1919. Germany had been defeated, but celebrations in the Allied nations were tempered with doubts about what the Great War had actually accomplished. The war had also generated disillusionment about the world in general. For example, prior to 1914 there had been widespread acceptance of the idea that economic and scientific progress would make war a thing of the past. But science and technology seemed only to have made the Great War more devastating than previous conflicts.

For those who wondered whether the fighting had been worth it, President Woodrow Wilson hoped to salvage more than just victory from the war. With his "Fourteen Points" peace proposal, Wilson hoped to address the flaws in the system of international diplomacy that had led to the war. Among Wilson's reforms were the abolition of secret treaties, a reduction of armaments, and the creation of a League of Nations that would work to preserve international law and prevent future wars.

Many Europeans embraced the Fourteen Points, and at the Paris Peace Conference, Wilson hoped to make them the basis for a peace treaty that all sides could endorse. However, both Great Britain and France opposed several of Wilson's proposals. Those two nations had been at war three years longer than the United States had; they had suffered more, and they were intent on punishing Germany. As a result Wilson was forced to compromise his vision of an equitable peace, and several punitive measures were incorporated to the final Treaty of Versailles. Germany was stripped of roughly 10 percent of its population and territory; it was permitted to keep only a very small standing army; and it was required to make compensation "for all damage done to the civilian population of the Allies and their property by the aggression of Germany by land, by sea and from the air." Perhaps most significant was the "war guilt clause" of the treaty, which explicitly blamed Germany for starting the war.

Wilson's Fourteen Points also faced opposition in the United States. Many congressmen objected to the fact that the Treaty of Versailles committed America to Wilson's proposed League of Nations. Isolationists (politicians who oppose committing the United States to other nations) feared that the League of Nations would

American troops are welcomed home during a parade in New York City after the end of World War I.

only end up entangling America in future European wars. Congress ultimately rejected the treaty: America did not participate in the postwar Allied reconstruction efforts, and the United States did not become a member of the League of Nations.

Historians generally agree that the harsh treatment of Germany in the Treaty of Versailles and the American rejection of the League of Nations paved the way for World War II. Adolf Hitler was able to institute his militaristic policies of the 1930s in part because of German resentment of the treaty's war guilt clause; without American support, the weakened League of Nations was unable to stop him. The documents in this chapter explore the aftermath of World War I and the imperfect peace it produced.

Blaming Germany for the War

In January 1919, the victorious Allied Powers appointed a fifteen-member commission to investigate who had been responsible for the start of the war. This is an excerpt from that group's 1919 report, which places primary blame on Germany and Austria-Hungary and secondary blame on the Ottoman Empire (Turkey) and Bulgaria. The report essentially reviews the events leading up to the outbreak of World War I, with emphasis on how Germany resisted other nations' attempts to avoid war.

On the question of the responsibility of the authors of the war, the Commission, after having examined a number of official documents relating to the origin of the World War, and to the violations of neutrality and of frontiers which accompanied its inception [beginning], has determined that the responsibility for it lies wholly upon the Powers which declared war in pursuance of a policy of aggression, the concealment of which gives to the origin of this war the character of a dark conspiracy against the peace of Europe.

This responsibility rests first on Germany and Austria, secondly on Turkey and Bulgaria. The responsibility is made all the graver by reason of the violation by Germany and Austria of the neutrality of Belgium and Luxembourg, which they themselves had guaranteed. It is increased, with regard to both France and Serbia, by the violation of their frontiers before the declaration of war.

Many months before the crisis of 1914 the German Emperor had ceased to pose as the champion of peace. Naturally believing in the overwhelming superiority of his Army, he openly showed his enmity [hostility] towards France. [German] General von Moltke said to the King of the Belgians: "This time the matter must be settled." In vain the King protested. The [German] Emperor and his Chief of Staff remained no less fixed in their attitude.

On the 28th of June, 1914, occurred the assassination at Sarajevo of the heir apparent of Austria. "It is the act of a little group of madmen," said [Emperor of Austria and King of Hungary] Francis Joseph. The act, committed as it was by a subject of Austria-Hungary on Austro-Hungarian territory, could in no wise [way] compromise Serbia, which very correctly expressed its condolences and stopped public rejoicings in Belgrade [Serbia]. If the Government of Vienna thought that there was any Serbian complicity, Serbia was ready to seek out the guilty parties. But this attitude failed to satisfy Austria and still less Germany, who, after their first astonishment had passed, saw in this royal and national misfortune a pretext to initiate war.

At Potsdam [Germany] a "decisive consultation" took place on the 5th of July, 1914. Vienna and Berlin decided upon this plan: "Vienna will send to Belgrade a very emphatic ultimatum with a very short limit of time."

The Bavarian [German] Minister, von Lerchenfeld, said in a confidential dispatch dated the 18th of July, 1914, the facts stated in which have never been officially denied: "It is clear that Serbia cannot accept the demands, which are inconsistent with the dignity of an independent state." Count Lerchenfeld reveals in this report that, at the time it was made, the ultimatum to Serbia had been jointly decided upon by the Governments of Berlin and Vienna; that they were waiting to send it until [French] President Poincaré and [French premier] Mr. [René] Viviani should have left for St. Petersburg [Russia]; and that no illusions were cherished, either at Berlin or

Vienna, as to the consequences which this threatening measure would involve. It was perfectly well known that war would be the result.

The Bavarian Minister explains, moreover, that the only fear of the Berlin Government was that Austria-Hungary might hesitate and draw back at the last minute, and that on the other hand Serbia, on the advice of France and Great Britain, might yield to the pressure put upon her. Now, "the Berlin Government considers that war is necessary." Therefore, it gave full powers to

General Helmuth Johannes Ludwig von Moltke of Germany.

Count Berchtold, who instructed the Ballplatz [a body of the Austro-Hungarian Government] on the 18th of July, 1914, to negotiate with Bulgaria to induce her to enter into an alliance and to participate in the war.

In order to mask this understanding, it was arranged that the Emperor should go for a cruise in the North Sea, and that the Prussian Minister of War should go for a holiday; so that the Imperial Government might pretend that events had taken it completely by surprise.

Austria suddenly sent Serbia an ultimatum that she had carefully prepared in such a way as to make it impossible to accept. Nobody could be deceived; "the whole world understands that this ultimatum means war." According to Mr. Sazonoff [the Russian foreign minister], "Austria-Hungary wanted to devour Serbia."

Mr. Sazonoff asked Vienna for an extension of the short time limit of forty-eight hours given by Austria to Serbia for the most serious decision in its history. Vienna refused the demand. On the 24th and 25th of July, England and France multiplied their efforts to persuade Serbia to satisfy the Austro-Hungarian demands. Russia threw in her weight on the side of conciliation.

Contrary to the expectation of Austria-Hungary and Germany, Serbia yielded. She agreed to all the requirements of the ultimatum, subject to the single reservation that, in the judicial inquiry which she would commence for the purpose of seeking out the guilty parties, the participation of

Count Leopold Anthony Johann Berchtold, Austro-Hungarian minister for foreign affairs, took part in negotiations with Bulgaria.

Austrian officials would be kept within the limits assigned by international law. "If the Austro-Hungarian Government is not satisfied with this," Serbia declared she was ready "to submit to the decision of the Hague Tribunal [an international court]."

"A quarter of an hour before the expiration of the time limit," at 5:45 on the 25th, Mr. Pashitch, the Serbian Minister for Foreign Affairs, delivered this reply to Baron Giesl, the Austro-Hungarian Minister.

On Mr. Pashitch's return to his own office he found awaiting him a letter from Baron Giesl saying that he was not satisfied with the reply. At 6:30 the latter had left Belgrade, and even before he had arrived at Vienna, the Austro-Hungarian Government had handed his passports to Mr. Yovanovitch, the Serbian Minister, and had prepared thirty-three mobilization proclamations, which were published on the following morning in the *Budapesti Kozloni*, the official gazette of the Hungarian Government. On the 27th Sir Maurice de Bunsen [the British Ambassador to Vienna] telegraphed to [British foreign minister] Sir Edward Grey: "This country has gone wild with joy at the prospect of war with Serbia." At midday on the 28th Austria declared war on Serbia. On the 29th the Austrian army commenced the bombardment of Belgrade and made its dispositions to cross the frontier.

The reiterated suggestions of the Entente Powers [the European Allies] with a view to finding a peaceful solution of the dispute only produced evasive replies on the part of Berlin or promises of intervention with the Government of Vienna without any effectual steps being taken.

On the 24th of July Russia and England asked that the Powers should be granted a reasonable delay in which to work in concert for the maintenance of peace. Germany did not join in this request.

On the 25th of July Sir Edward Grey proposed mediation by four Powers (England, France, Italy and Germany). France and Italy immediately gave their concurrence. Germany refused, alleging that it was not a question of mediation but of arbitration, as the conference of the four Powers was called to make proposals, not to decide.

On the 26th of July Russia proposed to negotiate directly with Austria. Austria refused.

On the 27th of July England proposed a European conference. Germany refused.

On the 29th of July Sir Edward Grey asked the Wilhelmstrasse [the German Government] to be good enough to "suggest any method by which the influence of the four Powers could be used together to prevent a war between Austria and Russia." She [Germany] was asked herself to say what she desired. Her reply was evasive.

British foreign minister Sir Edward Grey attempted to negotiate an alliance with Germany.

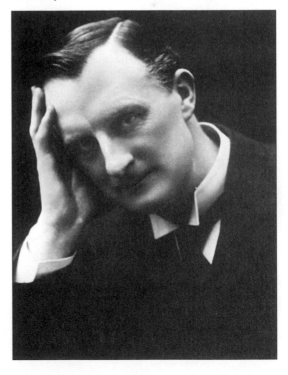

On the same day, the 29th of July, the [Russian] Czar [Nicholas II] dispatched to the Emperor William II [of Germany] a telegram suggesting that the Austro-Serbian problem should be submitted to the Hague Tribunal. This suggestion received no reply. This important telegram does not appear in the *German White Book*. It was made public by the Petrograd *Official Gazette* (January, 1915).

The Bavarian Legation, in a report dated the 31st of July, declared its conviction that the efforts of Sir Edward Grey to preserve peace would not hinder the march of events.

As early as the 21st of July German mobilization had commenced by the recall of a certain number of classes of the reserve, then of German officers in Switzerland, and finally of the Metz garrison on the 25th of July. On the 26th of July the German fleet was called back from Norway.

The Entente did not relax its conciliatory efforts, but the German Government systematically brought all its attempts to naught [nothing]. When Austria consented for the first time on the 31st of July to discuss the contents of the Serbian note with the Russian Government and the Austro-Hungarian Ambassador received orders to "converse" with the Russian Minister of Foreign Affairs, Germany made any negotiation impossible by sending her ultimatum to Russia. Prince Lichnowsky [a German diplomat] wrote that "a hint from Berlin would have been enough to decide Count Berchtold to content himself with a diplomatic success and to declare that he was satisfied with the Serbian reply, but this hint was not given. On the contrary they went forward towards war."

On the 1st of August the German Emperor addressed a telegram to the King of England containing the following sentence: "The troops on my frontier [border] are, at this moment, being kept back by telegraphic and telephonic orders from crossing the French frontier." Now, war was not declared till two days after that date, and as the German mobilization orders were issued on that same day, the 1st of August, it follows that, as a matter of fact, the German Army had been mobilized and concentrated in pursuance of previous orders.

The attitude of the Entente nevertheless remained still to the very end so conciliatory that, at the very time at which the German fleet was bombarding [the Russian port of] Libau, Nicholas II gave his word of honor to William II that Russia would not undertake any aggressive action during the pourparlers [discussions], and that when the German troops commenced their march across the French frontier Mr. Viviani telegraphed to all the French Ambassadors "we must not stop working for accommodation."

On the 3rd of August Mr. von Schoen [the German Ambassador to France] went to the Quai d'Orsay [the building that houses the French Ministry of Foreign Affairs] with the declaration of war against France. Lacking a real cause of complaint, Germany alleged, in her declaration of war, that bombs had been dropped by French

Nicholas II, czar of Russia, vowed to avoid all aggressive military action.

airplanes in various districts in Germany. This statement was entirely false. Moreover, it was either later admitted to be so or no particulars were ever furnished by the German Government.

Moreover, in order to be manifestly [clearly] above reproach, France was careful to withdraw her troops ten kilometers from the German frontier. Notwithstanding

this precaution, numerous officially established violations of French territory preceded the declaration of war.

The provocation was so flagrant that Italy, herself a member of the Triple Alliance, did not hesitate to declare that in view of the aggressive character of the war the *casus foederis* [the treaty Italy had signed with Germany and Austria-Hungary] ceased to apply.

Commission on the Responsibility of the Authors of the War and on the Enforcement of Penalties, *German White Book Concerning the Responsibility of the Authors of the War.* Trans. Carnegie Endowment for International Peace, 1919.

Woodrow Wilson's Fourteen Points

In this address given before Congress on January 8, 1918, President Woodrow Wilson announced his vision of the ground rules on which the Allies would consider peace with the Central Powers. Called the Fourteen Points, these became the basis on which the Allies eventually negotiated the Treaty of Versailles, the treaty that officially ended World War I.

We entered this war because violations of right had occurred which touched us to the quick and made the life of our own people impossible unless they were corrected and the world secure once and for all against their recurrence. What we demand in this war, therefore, is nothing peculiar to ourselves. It is that the world be made fit and safe to live in; and particularly that it be made safe for every peace-loving nation which, like our own, wishes to live its own

President Woodrow Wilson announces his Fourteen Points to Congress in an address on January 8, 1918.

life, determine its own institutions, be assured of justice and fair dealing by the other peoples of the world as against force and selfish aggression. All the peoples of the world are in effect partners in this interest, and for our own part we see very clearly that unless justice be done to others it will not be done to us. The program of the world's peace, therefore, is our program; and that program, the only possible program, as we see it, is this:

I. Open covenants of peace, openly arrived at, after which there shall be no private international understandings of any kind but diplomacy shall proceed always frankly and in the public view.

II. Absolute freedom of navigation upon the seas, outside territorial waters, alike in peace and in war, except as the seas may be closed in whole or in part by international action for the enforcement of international covenants.

III. The removal, so far as possible, of all economic barriers and the establishment of an equality of trade conditions among all the nations consenting to the peace and associating themselves for its maintenance.

IV. Adequate guarantees given and taken that national armaments [armed forces] will be reduced to the lowest point consistent with domestic safety.

V. A free, open-minded, and absolutely impartial adjustment of all colonial claims [claims to colonies in distant locations such as Africa and the Pacific], based upon a strict observance of the principle that in determining all such questions of sovereignty [authority over a country] the interests of the populations concerned must have equal weight with the equitable claims of the government whose title is to be determined.

VI. The [Central Powers'] evacuation of all Russian territory and such a settlement of all questions affecting Russia as will secure the best and freest cooperation of the other nations of the world in obtaining for her an unhampered and unembarrassed opportunity for the independent determination of her own political development and national policy and assure her of a sincere welcome into the society of free nations under institutions of her own choosing; and, more than a welcome, assistance also of every kind that she may need and may herself desire. The treatment accorded Russia by her sister nations in the months to come will be the acid test of their good will, of their comprehension of her needs as distinguished from their own interests, and of their intelligent and unselfish sympathy.

VII. Belgium, the whole world will agree, must be evacuated and restored, without any attempt to limit the sovereignty which she enjoys in common with all other free nations. No other single act will serve as this will serve to restore confidence among the nations in the laws which they have themselves set and determined for the government of their relations with one another. Without this healing act the whole structure and validity of international law is forever impaired.

VIII. All French territory should be freed and the invaded portions restored, and the wrong done to France by Prussia in 1871 in the matter of Alsace-Lorraine [a region of France taken by Germany (formerly Prussia) in 1871], which has unsettled the peace of the world for nearly fifty years, should be righted, in order that peace may once more be made secure in the interest of all.

IX. A readjustment of the frontiers [borders] of Italy should be effected along clearly recognizable lines of nationality.

X. The peoples of Austria-Hungary, whose place among the nations we wish to see safeguarded and assured, should be accorded the freest opportunity to autonomous [independent] development.

XI. Rumania [Romania], Serbia, and Montenegro should be evacuated; occupied territories restored; Serbia accorded free and secure access to the sea; and the relations of the several Balkan states to one another determined by friendly counsel along historically established lines of allegiance and nationality; and international guarantees of the political and economic independence and territorial integrity of the several Balkan states should be entered into.

XII. The Turkish portion of the present Ottoman Empire should be assured a secure sovereignty, but the other nationalities which are now under Turkish rule should be assured an undoubted security of life and an absolutely unmolested [free from interference] opportunity of autonomous development, and the Dardanelles [a strait in northwestern Turkey linking the Aegean Sea with the Sea of Marmara] should be permanently opened as a free passage to the ships and commerce of all nations under international guarantees.

XIII. An independent Polish state should be erected which should include the territories inhabited by indisputably Polish populations, which should be assured a free and secure access to the sea, and whose political and economic independence and territorial integrity should be guaranteed by international covenant.

XIV. A general association of nations must be formed under specific covenants for the purpose of affording mutual guarantees of political independence and territorial integrity to great and small states alike.

Woodrow Wilson, "Speech on the Fourteen Points," delivered, January 8, 1918, *Congressional Record*, 65th Cong., 2nd sess., 1918, pp. 680–81.

Concern over the Treaty of Versailles

Under the Treaty of Versailles, Germany was forced to admit sole blame for the war, disarm itself, commit to heavy reparation (compensation) payments to the Allies, and give up significant amounts of territory. Some observers, including the editors of the American magazine New Republic, *criticized the harsh terms of the treaty. Their concerns are expressed in the May 24, 1919, editorial reprinted below.*

In their comments on the Treaty of Versailles, the newspapers published in the Allied countries confine themselves chiefly to the expression of two sharply contrasted verdicts. Those which have vigorously supported the war praise the Treaty as a document, which, however harsh its terms may appear to be, is defensible as a stern but just attempt to make the punishment of Germany fit her crimes. Those which did not support the war or conditioned their support on the fulfillment of definite political objects are equally uncompromising in their rejection of the Treaty. They consider it a flagrant and perfidious [deceitful] repudiation of all the more generous, humane, and constructive objects in the name of which the people in the Allied countries were induced to shed their blood and sacrifice their lives.

A Third State of Mind

These hostile verdicts attract to themselves the limelight of public attention, but particularly in this country we should not overlook the third state of mind about the Treaty which is obtaining expression in some of the Western journals. There are many of our fellow countrymen, both in the East and in the

Representatives of the Allied nations draft the Treaty of Versailles. Many critics considered the terms of the treaty too harsh.

West, whose sense of justice and fair-dealing is outraged by the Treaty, but who cannot quite decide to place themselves in open and uncompromising opposition to it. Their state of mind is analogous to that of those Americans in August 1914 whose consciences were troubled by the wanton violence of the German invasion of Belgium, but who did not know how, as American citizens, they could assume effective responsibility for defeating the monster of militant imperialism.

To Americans who share this third state of mind, we should like to address an appeal. They are in danger now of committing a mistake similar to that which their fellow countrymen committed in the fall of 1914. During the early months of the war the majority of uneasy Americans compromised with their consciences. They usually became definitely pro-Ally in opinion, but they were mentally unprepared for war, and they considered it unnecessary to consider any method, short of an actual declaration of war, which would bring American political influence and economic power to the support of democratic Europe. In an analogous spirit, Americans who are deeply troubled by the proposed treaty of peace are feeling for a way out which does not imply outspoken and uncompromising opposition. Just as four and one-half years ago they shrank from breaking down the traditional aloofness of this country from European political and military controversies, so now they shrink from parting company with their recent companions in arms. The bonds forged by their fight against a common enemy are hard to break. If they reject the Treaty they are afraid of looking to themselves and to their European friends like quitters. They are longing for peace and are tempted to accept it at any price.

Yet if they connive [conspire] at this Treaty they will, as liberal and humane American democrats who seek by social experiment and education to render their country more worthy of its still unredeemed national promise, be delivering themselves into the hands of their enemies, the reactionaries and the revolutionists. The future of liberal Americanism depends upon a moral union between democracy and nationalism [devotion to one's own nation]. Such a union is compromised so long as nationalism remains competitive in policy, exclusive in spirit, and complacently capitalist in organization. Liberals all over the world have hoped that a war, which was so clearly the fruit of competition and imperialist and class-bound nationalism, would end in a peace which would moralize nationalism by releasing it from class bondage and exclusive ambitions.

An Inhuman Monster

The Treaty of Versailles does not even try to satisfy these aspirations. Instead of expressing a great recuperative [restorative] effort of the conscience of a civilization, which for its own sins has sweated so much blood, it does much to intensify and nothing to heal the old and ugly dissensions [conflicts] between political nationalism and social democracy. Insofar as its terms are actually carried out, it is bound to provoke the ultimate explosion of irreconcilable warfare. It weaves international animosities and the class conflict into the very fabric of the proposed new system of public law. The European politicians, who with American complicity have hatched this inhuman monster, have acted either cynically, hypocritically, or vindictively, and their handwork will breed cynicism, hypocrisy, or vindictiveness in the minds of future generations. The moral source of the political life of modern nations remains polluted.

The authors of the Treaty of Versailles are the victims of the blind interests and the imperious [domineering] determinism of an inhumane class economy. They admit in private conversation the diseased nature of their own offspring. "Even conservative opinion in Europe," says [journalist] William Allen White, "is frankly cynical about Germany's fulfillment of the terms imposed. They are too severe for Germany to live under for a generation. . . . They practically exterminate her as a nation." Why, then, did they do it? Why do they propose to terminate a war, fought in part to vindicate the sacredness of public treaties, by compelling the vanquished enemy to sign a bond which they know he cannot fulfill? The answer is not pleasant. They do this thing because they themselves are the unconscious servants of the cupidity [greed] and the vindictiveness which infect the psychology of an inhumane and complacent capitalist society.

They crave at any cost the emotional triumph of imposing on the German nation the ultimate humiliation of solemnly consenting to its own abdication as a self-governing and self-respecting community. To satisfy this craving they are so far as possible depriving the German people by public law of the status of economic citizens with rights which other nations are bound to respect. Thus they are deliberately raising the question of working class solidarity [unanimity of purpose]. They are defying the community of interest and the feeling of brotherhood which unites the socially alert workers of all the European peoples. They are subsidizing the growth of class-conscious and class-bound proletarian internationalism [union of world workers] dominated by the conviction of the incorrigible inhumanity of a capitalist national economy. They are demonstrating by example what a perfidious protectorate nationalism exercises over the common human interests of all peoples.

The Socialists [who advocate collective government ownership of all property] are fully alive to this deeper and less obvious meaning of the Treaty. They will flourish it as a complete vindication of the Marxian [revolutionary sociologist Karl Marx's] dogma that, as long as capitalism prevails, war necessarily operates as the instrument of class aggrandizement and popular exploitation.

The Treaty proposes the exploitation of the German people only, but an international organization whose chief object it is to profit by the exploitation of a subject people can survive only through the exploitation and deception of its own workers. The Treaty is, consequently, greeted as a declaration of a class war by organized society against the proletariat of all nations. It is condemned as a final exposure of the hypocrisy and inhumanity of a national economy.

Hitherto, in spite of all their propaganda and of the grievances of the wage-earning class, the Socialists have never persuaded the workers to believe in the need of a class war, or to undermine the popular confidence in nationalism. Now, as they believe, their class enemies have provided them with an unanswerable demonstration, and they are looking forward jubilantly to the inevitable revolution. The New York *Nation* announces confidently that all recent political and social convulsions are only "the preliminaries of the great revolution to whose support the friends of freedom must now rally everywhere."

A Decisive Test

In our opinion the Treaty of Versailles subjects all liberalism, and particularly that kind of liberalism which breathes the Christian spirit, to a decisive test. Its very life depends upon the ability of the modern national state to avoid the irreconcilable class conflict to which, as the Socialists claim, capitalism condemns the future of society. In the event of such a conflict, liberalism is ground, as it is being ground in Russia, between the upper and lower millstones [grinding forces] of re-action and revolution. The Treaty, insofar as it commits the national democracies to a permanent policy of inhumane violence, does weave this conflict into the fabric of international law. It is the most shameless and, we hope, the last of those treaties which, while they pretend to bring peace to a mortified world, merely write the specifications for future revolution and war. It presents liberalism with a perfect opportunity of proving whether or not it is actually founded in positive moral and religious conviction.

If a war which was supposed to put an end to war culminates [ends] without strenuous protest by humane men and women in a treaty of peace which renders peace impossible, the liberalism which preached this meaning for the war will have committed suicide. That such a protest on the part of national liberals may not have much immediate success in defeating the ratification of the Treaty is not essential. The Treaty of Versailles, no matter under what kind of compulsion it is ratified by the nations, is impossible of execution and will defeat itself.

But it is essential that the ratification should not take place with the connivance [acceptance] of the sincerely liberal and Christian forces in public opinion. For in that event national liberalism in the Allied countries will be following the example and inviting the fate of national liberalism in imperial Germany. It will become the dishonored accomplice of its own downfall. It will abandon society to an irresistible conflict between the immoral and intransigent [inflexible] forces of Junkerism [Prussian aristocracy] and revolutionary socialism.

The calamity of the war descended on the Western nations because of the existence of one crying weakness in Western civilization. The organized Christian nations could never agree upon an effective method of subordinating the exercise of political and economic power to moral and humane purposes. Many liberals have hoped that at the end of the war the enlightened conscience of the Western people would arise and exert itself to cure this weakness. The Treaty of Versailles is damned because it does nothing to moralize the future exercise of political and economic power. On the contrary, it conceives the victors who exercise the power as possessing only rights and the vanquished [defeated] who have lost the power as possessing only duties. The powerful are permitted to abuse it as much as they please, and, in their relations to the defeated Hungary, Austria, Russia, and Germany, they are encouraged and licensed to abuse it.

The past sins of the Hungarian and German ruling classes afford no justification for such a convenient and drastic system of future discrimination. Those who will not subordinate the exercise of power to rules of impartial justice sacrifice their moral right to inflict punishment. The Treaty does not embody either the spirit or method even of punitive justice. What it does embody and strain to the breaking point is the pagan doctrine and spirit of retaliation. What it treats with utter ignorance is the Christian doctrine of atonement and redemption. At a crisis in the history of civilization, the rulers of the victorious Christian states conclusively demonstrate their own contemptuous disbelief in the practical value of Christian moral economy.

The Treaty and the League

Just as the acceptance of the Treaty of Versailles without protest will undermine the moral foundation of nationalism and menace civilization with an uncontrollable class conflict, so its defeat or discredit will clearly and emphatically testify to a formative connection between religion and morals and economics and politics. It would begin the cure of the spiritual anarchy in Western civilization which the recent war and the proposed peace both exemplify. It would constitute the first step in the moral preparation of the Western democracies for a League of Nations.

For the possibility of any vital League of Nations does not depend, as so many liberals seem to suppose, on the ratification of the Treaty. It depends on the rejection of the Treaty. The League is not powerful enough to redeem the Treaty. But the Treaty is vicious enough to incriminate the League. It would convert the League into the instrument of competitive imperialist nationalism whose more disinterested members would labor in vain to mold it into a cooperative society. Liberal democrats cannot honestly consent to peace on the proposed terms. If it was wrong when confronted by the imperialist aggression of Germany to tolerate peace by conniving at such an attack, it is equally wrong when confronted by a treaty which organizes competitive imperialism into an international system to pay so high a price for the ending of the war. This above all others is the time and the occasion to repudiate [reject] the idea of peace at any price, to reject immediate peace at the price of permanent moral and economic warfare.

New Republic, May 24, 1919.

Opposition to the League of Nations

Although U.S. delegates signed the Treaty of Versailles at the Paris Peace Conference, there was considerable opposition to ratification of the treaty within the U.S. Congress. One reason for this opposition was "article 10" of the treaty, also known as the League of Nations Covenant, which committed the United States to joining the League of Nations, an international body that would work to prevent future wars. Although President Wilson considered the League of Nations to be his greatest achievement, many U.S. senators felt that inclusion in the league would entangle the United States in future foreign wars.

The leader of the opposition to the treaty was Senator Henry Cabot Lodge. In the August 12, 1919, address to Congress reprinted here, Lodge outlines the reasons he opposes the League of Nations. Ultimately the Treaty of Versailles failed to win ratification in the Senate, and the League of Nations was formed without the United States as a member.

I object in the strongest possible way to having the United States agree, directly or indirectly, to be controlled by a league which may at any time, and perfectly lawfully and in accordance with the terms of the covenant, be drawn in to deal with internal conflicts in other countries, no matter what those conflicts may be. We should never permit the United States to be involved in any internal conflict in another country, except by the will of her people expressed through the Congress which represents them.

Senator Henry Cabot Lodge led the opposition to the League of Nations.

Article 10

With regard to wars of external aggression on a member of the league, the case is perfectly clear. There can be no genuine dispute whatever about the meaning of the first clause of article 10. In the first place, it differs from every other obligation in being individual and placed upon each nation without the intervention of the league. Each nation for itself promises to respect and preserve as against external aggression the boundaries and the political independence of every member of the league. . . .

It is, I repeat, an individual obligation. It requires no action on the part of the league, except that in the second sentence the authorities of the league are to have the power to advise as to the means to be employed in order to fulfill the purpose of the first sentence. But that is a detail of execution, and I consider that we are morally and in honor bound to accept and act upon that advice. The broad fact remains that if any member of the league suffering from external aggression should appeal directly to the United States for support the United States would be bound to give that support in its own capacity and without reference to the action of other powers, because the United States itself is bound, and I hope the day will never come when the United States will not carry out its promises. If that day should come, and the United States or any other great country should refuse, no matter how specious [deceptively attractive] the reasons, to fulfill both in letter and spirit every obligation in this covenant, the United States would be dishonored and the league would crumble into dust, leaving behind it a legacy of wars. If China should rise up and attack Japan in an effort to undo the great wrong of the cession [relinquishing] of the control of Shantung [a province in northern China] to that power, we should be bound under the terms of article 10 to sustain Japan against China, and a guaranty of that sort is never involved except when the question has passed beyond the stage of negotiation and has become a question for the application of force. I do not like the prospect. It shall not come into existence by any vote of mine.

Henry Cabot Lodge, address to the U.S. Senate, August 12, 1919, *Congressional Record,* 66th Cong., 1st sess., pp. 3778–84.

Postwar Disillusionment Among Youth

In this 1920 Atlantic Monthly *article, American diplomat and writer John F. Carter Jr. discusses postwar disillusionment and loss of innocence among American youth. Carter comments that postwar attitudes about religion, women, and international peace after World War I became very different from what they were before the war. He suggests that the generation who grew up in the peaceful years before World War I were overly idealistic, but that his generation, who came into adulthood during the war, was forced to accept the sometimes harsh realities of the modern world. Nevertheless, Carter maintains that his generation is not cynical, but merely realistic.*

I would like to say a few things about my generation.

In the first place, I would like to observe that the older generation had certainly pretty well ruined this world before passing it on to us. They give us this Thing, knocked to pieces, leaky, red-hot, threatening to blow up; and then they are surprised that we don't accept it with the same attitude of pretty, decorous enthusiasm with which they received it, way back in the eighteen-nineties, nicely painted, smoothly running, practically foolproof. "So simple that a child can run it!" But the child couldn't steer it. He hit every possible telegraph-pole, some of them twice, and ended with a head-on collision for which we shall have to pay the fines and damages. Now, with loving pride, they turn over their wreck to us; and, since we are not properly overwhelmed with loving gratitude, shake their heads and sigh, "Dear! dear! We were so much better-mannered than these wild young people. But then we had the advantages of a good, strict, old-fashioned bringing-up!" How intensely human these oldsters are, after all, and how fallible! How they always blame us for not following precisely in their eminently correct footsteps!

Then again there is the matter of outlook. When these sentimental old world-wreckers were young, the world was such a different place. . . . Life for them was bright and pleasant. Like all normal youngsters, they had their little tin-pot ideals, their sweet little visions, their naive enthusiasms, their nice little sets of beliefs. Christianity had emerged from the blow dealt by [naturalist

Charles] Darwin, emerged rather in the shape of social dogma. Man was a noble and perfectible creature. Women were angels (whom they smugly sweated in their industries and prostituted in their slums). Right was downing might. The nobility and the divine mission of the race were factors that led our fathers to work wholeheartedly for a millennium, which they caught a glimpse of just around the turn of the century. Why, there were Hague Tribunals [international courts]! International peace was at last assured, and according to current reports, never officially denied, the American delegates held out for the use of poison gas in warfare, just as the men of that generation were later to ruin [President Woodrow] Wilson's great ideal of a league of nations, on the ground that such a scheme was an invasion of American rights. But still, everything, masked by ingrained hypocrisy and prudishness, seemed simple, beautiful, inevitable.

Now my generation is disillusioned, and, I think, to a certain extent, brutalized, by the cataclysm which their complacent folly [foolishness] engendered. The acceleration of life for us has been so great that into the last few years have been crowded the experiences and the ideas of a normal lifetime. We have in our unregenerate [unreformed] youth learned the practicality and the cynicism that is safe only in unregenerate old age. We have been forced to become realists overnight, instead of idealists, as was our birthright. We have seen man at his lowest, woman at her lightest, in the terrible moral chaos of Europe. We have been forced to

question, and in many cases to discard, the religion of our fathers. We have seen hideous peculation [government corruption], greed, anger, hatred, malice, and all uncharitableness, unmasked and rampant and unashamed. . . . We have seen the rottenness and shortcomings of all governments, even the best and most stable. We have seen entire social systems overthrown, and our own called in question. In short, we have seen the inherent beastliness of the human race revealed in an infernal apocalypse.

It is the older generation who forced us to see all this, which has left us with social and political institutions staggering blind in the fierce white light that, for us, should beat only about the enthroned ideal. . . .

We are faced with staggering problems and are forced to solve them, while the previous incumbents are permitted a graceful and untroubled death. All my friends are working and working hard. Most of the girls I know are working. In one way or another, often unconsciously, the great burden put upon us is being borne, and borne gallantly. . . . A keen interest in political and social problems, and a determination to face the facts of life, ugly or beautiful, characterizes us, as it certainly did not characterize our fathers. We won't shut our eyes to the truths we have learned. We have faced so many unpleasant things already—and faced them pretty well—that it is natural that we should keep it up.

Now I think that this is the aspect of our generation that annoys the uncritical and deceives the unsuspecting oldsters who are now met in judgment upon us: our devastating and brutal frankness. And this is the quality in which we really differ from our predecessors. We are frank with each other, frank, or pretty nearly so, with our elders, frank in the way we feel toward life and this badly damaged world. It may be a disquieting and misleading habit, but is it a bad one? We find some few things in the world that we like, and a whole lot that we don't, and we are not afraid to say so or to give our reasons. In earlier generations this was not the case. The young men yearned to be glittering generalities, the young women to act like shy, sweet, innocent fawns—toward one another. And now, when grown up, they have come to believe that they actually were figures of pristine excellence, knightly chivalry, adorable modesty, and impeccable propriety. But I really doubt if they were so.

John F. Carter Jr., "These Wild Young People (by One of Them)," *Atlantic Monthly,* September 1920.

Cooperation Was Necessary for Victory

Captain B. H. Liddell Hart was a leading British military strategist and historian who served as a tank commander during World War I. In this excerpt from his 1930 book, The Real War, 1914–1918, *he summarizes his view of the reasons for the final Allied victory. Hart refuses to credit any one development as the decisive element that brought victory. Instead he develops his view that World War I marked the beginning of a new type of warfare,* one that required the mobilization not only of mass armies, navies, and air forces, but also entire political systems, economies, cultures, and civilian populations.

The truth is that no one cause was, or could be, decisive. The western front, the Balkan front, the tank, the blockade, and propaganda have all been claimed as the cause of victory. All claims are justified; none is wholly right, although the blockade ranks first and began first. In this warfare between nations, victory is a cumulative effect, to which all weapons— military, economic, and psychological— contribute. Victory comes, and can only come, through the utilization and combination of all the resources existing in a modern nation, and the dividend of success depends on the way in which these manifold [diverse] activities are coordinated.

It is even more futile to ask which country won the war. France did not win the war, but unless she had held the fort while the forces of Britain were preparing, and those of America still a dream, the release of civilization from this nightmare of militarism would have been impossible. Britain did not win the war, but without her command of the sea, her financial support, and her army to take over the main burden of the struggle from 1916 onwards, defeat would have been inevitable. The United States did not win the war, but without their economic aid to ease the strain, without the

American officers and soldiers rest near the ruins of a house in France.

arrival of their troops to turn the numerical balance, and above all, without the moral tonic which their coming gave, victory would have been impossible. And let us not forget how many times Russia had sacrificed herself to save her Allies; preparing the way for their ultimate victory as surely as for her own downfall. Finally, whatever be the verdict of history on her policy, unstinted [plentiful] trib-

ute is due to the incomparable endurance and skill with which Germany more than held her own for four years against superior numbers—an epic of military and human achievement.

B. H. Liddell Hart, *The Real War, 1914–1918.* London: Faber & Faber, 1930.

✯ Chronology of Events ✯

June 28, 1914

Archduke Franz Ferdinand assassinated in Sarajevo.

August 4, 1914

President Woodrow Wilson formally proclaims American neutrality in the war.

February 4, 1915

Germany declares a war zone around the British Isles to begin on February 18.

February 10, 1915

The State Department formally protests the German declaration of a war zone.

April 11, 1915

The German ambassador to the United States calls on Americans to stop exporting arms to the Allies.

May 7, 1915

A German submarine sinks the British passenger liner *Lusitania* without warning. One hundred and twenty-eight Americans die.

June 3, 1916

Congress enacts the National Defense Act, authorizing a five-year expansion of the American army to 223,000 and establishing officer training programs in universities.

July 30, 1916

An explosion at a munitions plant on Black Tom Island in New Jersey is one of several incidents attributed to German sabotage.

August 31, 1916

Germany announces a suspension of submarine attacks.

November 17, 1916

Wilson, campaigning on a "He kept us out of war" slogan, is reelected to a second term.

January 16, 1917

German foreign minister Arthur Zimmermann sends a coded telegram to the German minister in Mexico proposing a German-Mexican military alliance.

January 31, 1917

Germany resumes unrestricted submarine warfare; three days later, the United States breaks off diplomatic relations with Germany.

March 1, 1917

The State Department reveals the contents of the Zimmermann telegram, which had been intercepted by British agents, to the American press.

March 15, 1917

Czar Nicholas II of Russia abdicates. A provisional government takes power, but its authority is undercut by the Petrograd Soviet, a council that calls on Russian soldiers to prepare for internal revolution.

April 2, 1917
Wilson asks Congress for a declaration of war against Germany; America enters the war four days later following congressional approval.

April 14, 1917
Wilson establishes the Committee on Public Information; it is charged with rallying American public opinion behind the war.

June 16, 1917
Congress passes the Espionage Act.

June 26, 1917
The first American troops arrive in France.

November 7, 1917
The Bolsheviks, led by Vladimir Lenin and Leon Trotsky, seize power in Russia.

January 18, 1918
Wilson delivers his "Fourteen Points" address to Congress, describing his vision of an American peace program.

March 21, 1918
Germany launches the Somme offensive; the Lys and Aisne offensives follow in April and May.

June/July 1918
American soldiers engage in their first major battles at Belleau Wood and Château-Thierry in France.

July 1918
American soldiers play a major role in the Second Battle of the Marne.

September 12, 1918
American soldiers launch the Saint Mihiel offensive; they take fifteen thousand German prisoners.

September 26, 1918
The Meuse-Argonne offensive begins. It is the final Allied offensive, and it continues until the end of the war.

November 11, 1918
An armistice ending the fighting of World War I is reached after Germany asks for peace on the basis of Wilson's Fourteen Points.

January 25, 1919
Delegates to the Paris Peace Conference formally approve Wilson's request that the League of Nations be made an integral part of the peace treaty.

June 28, 1919
The Treaty of Versailles is signed by Germany and the Allies.

November 19, 1919
By a vote of 55-39, the U.S. Senate rejects the Treaty of Versailles.

November 2, 1920
Republican Warren G. Harding is elected president; his election signals America's rejection of Wilson's dreams of a new international order.

☆ Index ☆

American position on, 7
argument against, 21–24
argument for 15–19
Taft on, 15–19
Wilson on, 18–19
New York Tribune (newspaper), 49–53
Nicholas II (czar of Russia), 74
"Not Our War" (Reed), 54–58

One Man's Initiation—1917 (Dos Passos), 34
"Over There" (song), 53–54

pacifists, 48
Paris Peace Conference, 68, 83
Pershing, John J., 42–44, 46
pilots, 38–40
Poincaré, Raymond, 71
poison gas
  described by Dos Passos, 34–35
  introduction of, 28
  use of, at Ypres, 32–34
prejudice, 64–65
prisoners of war, 41–42
propaganda, 23, 48, 58–59
Prussia. *See* Germany

racism, 64–65
railroads, 31–32, 48
railways. *See* railroads
Randolph, Asa Philip, 64–65
rationing, 48
Real War, 1914–1918, The (Hart), 87–88
reconstruction, 70

Red Air Fighter, The (von Richthofen), 38–40
Red Baron, 38–40
Red Cross, 48
Reed, John, 54–58
Richthofen, Manfred von, 38–40
Rickenbacker, Eddie, 44–46
Russia
  alliance with France and, 7, 71
  alliance with Great Britain and, 7
  Bolshevik revolution in, 62
  1914 peace efforts of, 73
  as protector of Serbia, 7
  secret alliance against, 10

Saint-Mihiel, Battle of, 42–46
Sarajevo, 7, 70–71
  see also Franz Ferdinand
Schlieffen Plan, 12
Sedition Act, 49, 60–62
segregation, 64–65
Serbia, 7, 71, 72–73
shellshock, 28
ships, 26
Socialist Party of America, 62
socialists, 48, 54–58, 62–64, 81–82
Soldier's Life, A (McDonald), 47
songs, 52, 53–54
Storm of Steel: From the Diary of a German Storm-Troop Officer on the Western Front (Junger), 46–47
submarines, 8, 19–21, 24, 26–27

Swanwick, Helen, 65–67

Taft, William Howard, 15–18
tanks, 28
These Wild Young People (by One of Them) (Carter), 85–87
treaties, 9–10, 11
  see also names of specific agreements or countries
Treaty of Versailles
  arguments against adoption of treaty terms, 78–83
  "Article 10" League of Nations Covenant and, 83
  as based on Fourteen Points, 75
  capitalism and, 81–82
  Christianity and, 82–83
  class warfare and, 81–83
  German treatment in, 68–69, 78
  imperialism and, 83
  League of Nations and, 83
  liberalism and, 81–82
  nationalism and, 83
  opposition to U.S. signing of, 83–85
  Socialist movement and, 81–82
  war guilt clause, 69–70
  see also Fourteen Points
trench warfare
  disadvantages of, 30–31
  hardships of, 28–32, 34–36
  necessity for, 30–31
  skill of German army at, 32
Triple Alliance. *See* Central Powers

⋆ Picture Credits ⋆

☆ About the Editor ☆

James D. Torr has edited numerous books for Greenhaven Press and Lucent Books. He currently works as a freelance editor in Providence, Rhode Island.